Old Niagara on the Lake

University
of Toronto
Press

Peter John Stokes

Old Niagara on the Lake

drawings by Robert Montgomery

The houses are in general composed of wood, and have a neat and clean appearance; their present number may amount to near two hundred. The streets are spacious, and laid out at right angles to each other, so that the town when completed will be healthful and airy.
GEORGE HERIOT
Travels through the Canadas
London 1807

Excepting Brockville, it is the neatest Village in the Province and, on account of its healthy situation and proximity to the falls of Niagara has become a fashionable place of resort, during the summer months.
EDWARD ALLEN TALBOT
Five Years' Residence in the Canadas
London 1824

I asked for a bookseller's shop; there is not one in the town, but plenty of taverns ...
ANNA BROWNELL JAMESON
Winter Studies and Summer Rambles in Canada
London 1838

© University of Toronto Press 1971
Toronto and Buffalo
Printed in Canada
Reprinted 1977, 1980
ISBN 0-8020-1773-8
ISBN (paper) 0-8020-6318-7
LC 74-151393

Affectionately to J.J.

Contents

Preface

The purpose of this book is to reach people; and it may do this in several ways. For those who have never enjoyed the sights of this remarkable community with its wealth of early buildings expressing our own history, this may be an introduction. For those who have savoured it but not yet fully appreciated its worth, perhaps it will be an encouragement to delve further, to spend more time, to look again. And to anyone thoroughly familiar with the scene may it renew the sense of pride such a community should engender, and imbue its citizens with delight and joy in that calm of continuity from generations past, the magic of our short history so aptly expressed by Jeanne Minhinnick in the phrase 'the hand that touched the hand that touched the hand.'

What, of course, it does not purport to be is an authoritative and complete historic narrative of the town; it is more the architectural story in contemporary terms of a selection of the early buildings chosen to represent a number of different aspects and periods of the town's social background. On the basis of such a selection anyone wanting to make his personal survey can pick up other fascinating material – and this book is intended to whet the appetite.

The material included is a variety; some buildings are architecturally significant in their own right, others fill in the background. The total creates a range of building, the products of the tradesmen of the day, many of whom were superior craftsmen leaving behind them exquisite samples of their work for our use and pleasure.

Both for brevity of the text and emphasis upon visual appreciation the historic aspect has been curtailed. For easier comprehension of the earlier buildings Robert Montgomery has practised some graphic editing in his drawings: where essential features have been lost and can be re-established by investigation or reasonable conjecture these have been in-cluded, for it would be violating the reader's sensibility not to do so. The eye naturally tends to leave out modern impedimenta for it has the ability both to focus and to filter as it becomes more familiar, and more experienced – something the camera can never accomplish without mechanical or optical adjustment. The camera in this case serves a special purpose as our spyglass to concentrate in the glossary upon the delight of detail, a delight captured by Philip Shackleton.

It is wise to mention here an episode that proves that conjecture can be far from infallible, despite one's experience. The drawing for the Moore-Bishop-Stokes House (48) is based upon a sketch made prior to recent preservation work and before detailed examination revealed evidence contrary to supposition. The facts now point to the north room, previously assumed to be an addition, as the original kitchen to the house and part of the main building while the small chimney amidships proves to be later and constructed of hand-made brick salvaged from the old cooking fireplace and bakeoven.

A note about nomenclature is perhaps relevant because the technique often varies from place to place. Here consistency is attempted by giving the name of the original owner first, the present owner second, and mentioning any inconsistencies where these occur. Where the second name is omitted it is usually because the house has never been known otherwise. Where inn names are prominently connected with the buildings these are mentioned, while later titles have been appended where they are still in common local usage. Where house titles include three names this is a concession to a local family well known in connection with the building as its owners for over half a century. Ownerships, and therefore the names we have used here, do change; those recorded are accurate to January 1971.

The dating of buildings in most cases is approximate for documentation is scarce: therefore, in the initial choice the author was left to the limitations of his own experience. Records such as deeds were checked and in the search of title corroboration was often found in the increased value represented in a particular transaction, or the registering of a mortgage which could suggest a building operation. Only occasionally is the date recorded – on a datestone, in a letter, or some other reference that has come down to us – and such confirmation is mentioned where applicable.

The order of presentation of the buildings was chosen for convenience, and particularly for those who may wish to make a visit to old Niagara-on-the-Lake; a scheme of three separate tours has been evolved, beginning and ending with the Niagara Apothecary. The first tour, including buildings 1 to 38, traverses a large section of the older part of the town. The second tour includes buildings 39 to 48 and covers much of the New Survey. The third tour, with buildings 49 to 58, is intended to reach also the main historic sites, the three principal churches of interest, and the Niagara Historical Society Museum. Tours may be taken in whole or in part, in either direction as your wish, inclination, or stamina allows.

This then is the reason and the reasoning behind this modest attempt to present what has come down to us in one small town, almost two centuries old and still alive.

P.J.S.
Niagara-on-the-Lake
January 1971

Acknowledgments

It is with many thanks that the author wishes to acknowledge the help of those who contributed to the historical background of this book: the Dominion Archives and National Library, Ottawa, particularly the staff in the map division; the Province of Ontario Department of Public Records and Archives, Toronto; the Toronto Public Library, in particular the reference section and historical collections; the Registry Office of Niagara North (formerly the County of Lincoln), St Catharines, Ontario; and, in Niagara-on-the-Lake, The Niagara Historical Society, Mrs Frances MacKay, and last, but no means least, my wife, Ann, who by perseverance doggedly unravelled the secrets of deeds and other information.

My thanks go to those who by design and encouragement have laid some foundation even long ago, and kindred spirits who made the effort even more worthwhile: John Ansell Stokes who took his young boy by the hand to see old buildings; Jacobine Jones, RCA, who during the formative years fostered an interest that came to be lasting; Dr Eric R. Arthur and Professor Anthony P.C. Adamson, stars of college memories; Jack Herbert, who as Chief of Historic Sites in 1962 lifted the bushel from Niagara's light; A.J.H. Richardson, Architectural Historian with the National Historic Sites Services; Verschoyle B. Blake, Consultant to the Ontario Department of Public Records and Archives, for his encouragement and, in particular, his help in matters historical; Mrs Jeanne Minhinnick, partner in the most enjoyable escapades in restoration and preservation at Upper Canada Village and since; Mrs Cyril Inderwick, for related inspiration; Miss Audrey Spencer, colleague in the Carman House caper; and all those who so coolly, calmly, and kindly took a new Canadian and tried to give him the grass roots he lacked: the Cunningham family of Morrisburg, Ontario, and others in New Brunswick who did likewise.

With thanks and respects too to those organi-

7 zations and persons in Niagara-on-the-Lake who try hard to preserve the unique collection of early buildings, changing only sympathetic-ally while ensuring their enjoyment and use, most particularly: The Niagara Foundation, its President, Gerald R. Wooll, and Directors; Harry B. Picken, P.Eng.; and the newcomers, represented by such people as John Downton and Paul Firlotte. And finally and especially many thanks to Mrs Kathleen Courtney, my secretary, for her patient assistance in typing a scrawl into a legible script.

The plan of Niagara on pages 8 and 9 and the drawings of the Smith house and the two Dickson houses on page 10 are repro-duced with the permission of the Public Archives of Canada. The photograph of Queen street on page 13 is reproduced with permission from a copy of a photograph belonging to the Niagara Historical Society.

Introduction

History begins in some remote time so far as people are concerned, but when history is written it becomes record, a foundation of fact rebuilt constantly by interpretation. And, if one is so inclined, many lifetimes could be spent gathering facts and many more wasted trying to sort out fact and fiction or fact from the interpretation that pervades all local his-tories.

We are more concerned here with the imme-diate history of Niagara-on-the-Lake, the essential, recorded facts of its physical form as we now see it and comparisons, perhaps, with former times. This history is a relatively brief period of some two centuries, or roughly seven generations. The War of Independence fought by the American colonies is, effec-tively, the start of our story. It was a struggle for local autonomy, for a measure of freedom from what seemed to be autocracy from afar; it is the natural reaction of people to feel fet-terless, to want to determine their own destiny as a growing society, especially one capable of doing so economically. It was a civil war too, of internal factions, and the country was di-vided. Many of those loyal to the Crown, grateful for the institutions connected with it or feeling more secure in the tradition it represented – and some, perhaps, recogniz-ing greater opportunity on a new frontier – moved on, either east or north into the bor-dering lands beyond the thirteen rebellious colonies. Others left for the West Indies or returned to England.

The move seems to have been a gradual one, the border at first ill-defined even though natural barriers seemed to be an obvious place to draw the line. Late in the eighteenth century, just after the conclusion of the War, it was clear that Fort Niagara had to be abandoned and shop set up on the western side of the Niagara River. Simply put, so Upper Canada began, a place for the Loyal-ists to settle once again under the British Crown. The land was surveyed and conveyed to those who sought it or were considered worthy of it because of their attitude.

In 1792 the governor of the new colony, Colonel John Graves Simcoe, saw the need for immediate arrangements to deal with the influx of people, to organize the government to deal with the myriad problems that settlement produced. The most convenient and accessible place at the time was this crossing of the border, where so many settlers had already gathered. Newark was made the capital of Upper Canada, the first, temporary, location. Its former names of West Niagara, Lenox, and Butlersburg were abandoned; by the end of the century the lovelier sounding Oniaghara (pronounced O-ni-a-ga-ra) was transcribed as Niagara and finally, to avoid postal confusion, the town became Niagara-on-the-Lake toward the end of the nineteenth century.

The former administrative districts were divided into counties, townships were surveyed and divided into lots, settlers moved in to clear the land and farm. A military reserve was set apart and a site designated near the mouth of the Niagara River for the new Fort George, named in honour of George III, to replace that relinquished on the other side. In 1791 a Town plot had been devised with generous street allowances, those now named King, Queen, Mary, William, Mississauga, and Butler were a chain and a half (ninety-nine feet), the remainder a chain, or sixty-six feet, wide. The layout was the work of military minds, a gridiron of four-acre blocks subdivided into one-acre lots, like a Roman camp. Subsequently the part between Queen and the waterfront was divided into half-acre parcels and in 1794 the plot was enlarged to a plan of 412 lots including reserves. An area for a town centre was left toward the interior; perversely it grew up along Queen street at a more convenient location, closer to the fort, the waterfront, and town building as it actually took place. Clergy reserves were set out for the churches. Government, governor, and family were installed in hastily converted

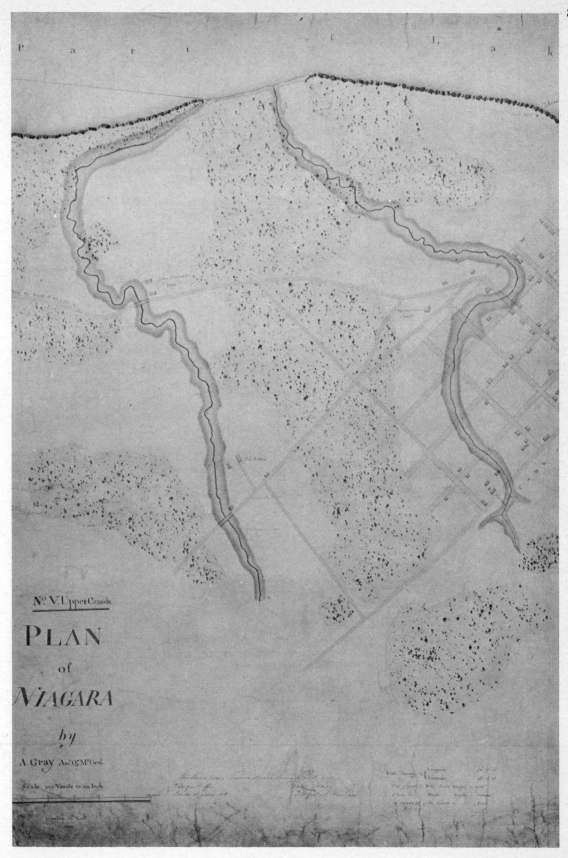

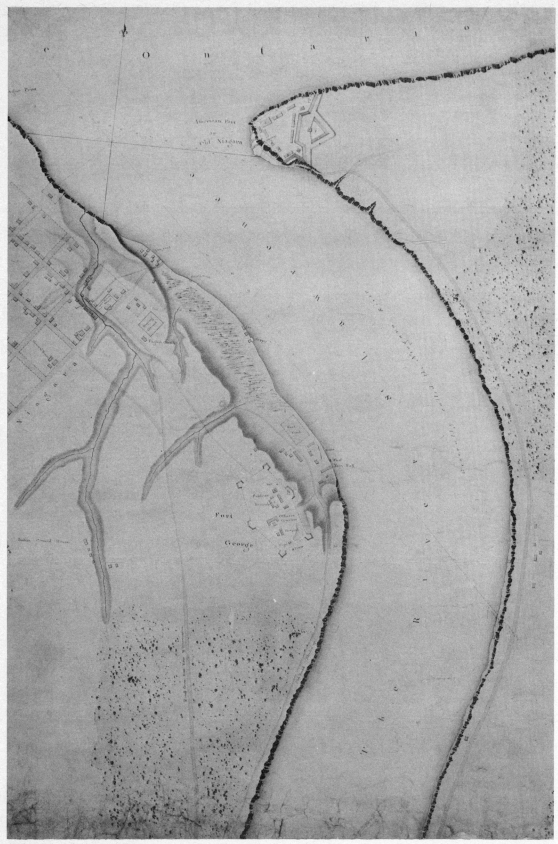

9

naval storehouses; one which is believed to have been part of this complex is still known as Navy Hall and stands near the waterfront below Fort George. Construction of the fort began, to be carried on more vigorously after 1795.

Appointed officials congregated as government began in 1792; Newark almost overnight became a court. A society had been transplanted there, complete with all the customs and accoutrements, and demands for company and service were met as townspeople settled in. Governmental and military demands encouraged commercial enterprise; Niagara's position on the lake – the principal transportation route and virtually the only one at the time – guaranteed a certain measure of success. In 1794 D.W. Smith, deputy surveyor general, reports about 150 houses, and Christian Schultz notes in his travels of 1807 and 1808 that the town then contained some 200 houses.

Tastes and traditions well ingrained obviously sought expression as the fruits of prosperity, the assumption of position, and the satisfaction of people's natural tendency to display came foremost. And we gather from descriptions and graphic records there were apparently opportunities to build grandly and craftsmen to oblige. It is recorded that even tradesmen from Lower Canada were employed in early building, to satisfy the growing demands. No doubt others already trained made their way to the new capital or came as settlers to the area.

There were fine buildings of the Georgian tradition as well as those exhibiting Regency tendencies in the early town: the claims of those who lost their houses in the War of 1812 attest to this. Churches too were built, but only St Mark's has survived in part from the early period.

Plan of Niagara 1810 by A. Gray
Assistant Quartermaster General, Quebec

However, the status of the town changed early as Governor Simcoe sought a position less vulnerable to unfriendly attack, and in 1797 York was selected as the new capital, despite Simcoe's preference for London. Newark was no longer the seat of central government but it still retained an important role as the district headquarters for this part of the colony. There was still much travel to and fro, and Newark, or Niagara as it soon came to be called, continued to prosper. Not long afterwards Governor Simcoe's fears were proved to have been well founded as the iniquitous, and for the principal combatants ignominous, War of 1812 commenced. This is 'the' War in the town's history, the single event which, combined with circumstance, produced Niagara-on-the-Lake as we now know it.

The Niagara frontier was the scene of most of the activity in the War of 1812, the line moving forwards and backwards as the Americans pushed their opportunity and the King's forces and their Loyalist companions fought back. The death of General Sir Isaac Brock at the Battle of Queenston Heights in October 1812 was a sad blow to the morale of the army and the colony at the time, for he had proved able and popular. Then the Americans occupied the Town, from late May to early December 1813, living for a time no doubt in a taut atmosphere of suspicion and distaste, but the townspeople managed to carry on. Turning fortunes, however, prompted the Americans to withdraw, and on the cold, windy winter day of 10 December 1813 the inhabitants, mostly older people, women, and children who had stayed behind, were told to leave their houses while the enemy set fire to the town. In return the settlements along the American side of the Niagara River were put to the torch following the capture of Fort Niagara by the British shortly afterwards. A similar fate had befallen the new capital

These houses were burned in 1813 and the drawings are part of the war losses claims.

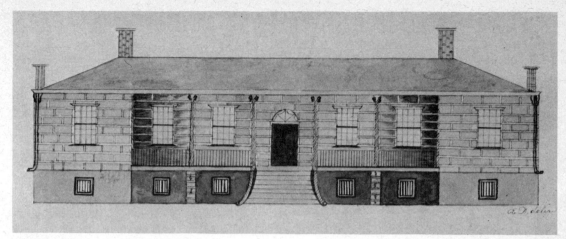

William Dickson house c1810

D.W. Smith house 1794

William Dickson house c1794

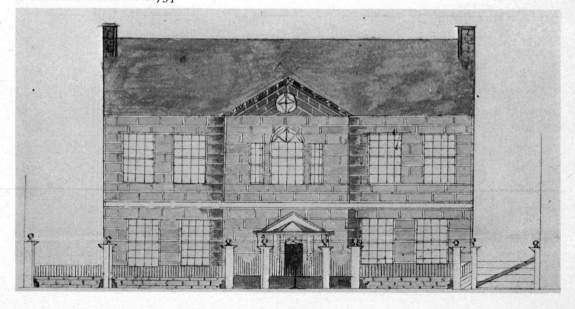

York; in reprisal it is said the British burnt Washington in the following year and the smoke-stained President's residence had to be painted, to be called forever after the White House.

The act was a cruel one, some say unjustified, but all seems fair in such circumstances. The government soon became involved in claims for destroyed property and, in the case of Niagara, recommended relocation of the town. The inhabitants who had drifted back refused and the phoenix arose from the ashes in the ensuing years. Some reorganizing of the function of the town did come about, however. Recognizing the vulnerable position of the Court House on lower King directly in view of Fort Niagara and within easy range of its guns, the new Court House proposed in 1816 was placed at the other end of King street! At the foot of King, at the water's edge, the Customs House and the early newspaper office were rebuilt. Commercial enterprises tended to become concentrated on the first wide street along Queen, except those directly connected with shipping and needing to be near the waterfront. The residential quarter sprang up in between and also around Queen, with a string of houses towards the new Court House. Front and Prideaux, Queen and Johnson, with the cross streets from King to Mississauga, were the earliest to be rebuilt, with isolated buildings placed elsewhere in the town plot. The building of Fort Mississauga required yet another reserve and the property of the Honourable James Crooks was confiscated in exchange for lands east of King. The streets beyond King, therefore, were given different names from those to the west when the 'new' survey was opened up after the War.

Fort Mississauga, the star-shaped earthwork with keep-like central structure on the lakefront, had been proposed before the War to guard and survey the approaches to Niagara at the mouth of the river. Its form is often stated to be unique; it has also been considered militarily indefensible and very vulnerable. Never has it fired a shot at an enemy or in anger. Its brickwork tower is said to have been built from the rubble of the town after the burning of 1813, and its heterogenous nature and stucco finish may well support this tale. Some early plans show that a much more elaborate scheme was once proposed. For all intents and purposes it appears to have been redundant, but built to placate an outraged populace; so it survives as a crumbling monument to the political placebo.

Niagara from the outset had been the end of a slave railway and many coloured families settled in the town. For many years the area not far from the Negro Burial Ground near Mary and Mississauga and principally along Mary was known locally as Niggertown, a name no longer considered acceptable. Many of the smaller and older houses of this part of town may well have belonged to negro families, but now all their descendants have moved away. The Baptist Church was built beside the Negro Burial Ground in 1831; it is said to have been moved away to become a barn.

The commercial centre continued to prosper; Niagara still enjoyed mercantile pre-eminence at the end of Lake Ontario and as the headquarters of the district. In 1824 a rattle of doom was heard: the sod for the first Welland Canal was turned. St Catharine's, Niagara's rival on the new waterway, and with a source of power available for industry, began to grow; the tug of war became evident. But the first canal, though a working model, was hardly a serious threat and Niagara's prosperity was not yet harmed, its sun barely overshadowed. The Niagara Dock Company, founded in 1831, proved a boon to the town, this new industry obviously contributing to its continuing prosperity. This may be reflected in the significant rise in population of the early 1840s, for by the 1850s the dock company's establishment was quite substantial with a great many buildings and workshops. Other industries not dependent on water power gathered along the waterfront: they included a tannery and a brewery using the copious spring water. A map of 1835 shows Fort George as being in ruins even though much of its fortifications had survived the War.

In the 1830s a significant wave of immigration had reached Upper Canada. By the 1840s this was swelled by those fleeing from the dreadful potato famine in Ireland and many came to Niagara in the hope of finding work and opportunity or to labour on the second Welland Canal and later on the construction of the railroad. Some people in Niagara still refer to the south-east sector of the town, an area of high flat land dotted with a number of smaller and older buildings not far from the second Court House, as 'Irishtown.' Perhaps this is where the Irish congregated; probably the land was cheaper and it was certainly not much built upon at the time.

The second Welland Canal, opened in the mid 1840s, spelt the doom of Niagara as a port and as a commercial centre; henceforward it was to retire with the relics of its prosperous past clustered around it, never to see the sought-after link with the new water way. Off the track, away from newer poles of development, it languished; but, being substantially built, it survived. The temporary rise in population appears to have been accommodated in smaller buildings or extensions to older ones: there is little to demonstrate any grand concept or plan at the time. Desperately trying to save its last remaining link as a seat of government, Niagara built a new Court House in 1847, to the designs of the architect, William Thomas, and on a site in the commercial area on Crown land which had been deeded for Town purposes, but was subsequently partly built on by private entrepreneurs. Within two decades Lincoln county had moved its headquarters to St Catharines, and Niagara now had only the intermittently occupied military camp, faltering industries, and its own populace to sustain it.

During this period the Free Kirk was set up as a faction of the Presbyterians. Their place of worship, now known as Grace United Church on Victoria street near Queen, was built in 1852, to the designs of William Thomas, architect of the Court House. Upon reunion in 1875 the Methodists took over the building, abandoning their 1823 meeting house, which was considered too costly to maintain, but was subsequently moved to survive to this day as a house.

The Dock Company continued for a time. And in 1854 the railway constructed between Chippawa and Queenston around the Falls in 1838 was to be extended to the mouth of the Niagara River, to thunder down King street to the waterside by 1862. This, with the increase in steamer traffic on the lake, again put Niagara on transportation routes, but it was still a long way off the beaten path. It did serve, however, to lay the foundation for its revival as one of the principal resort areas of the late nineteenth century, a place on the water, where fresh air and a moderate climate second to none in the province might be enjoyed in peace and relative economy. The network of electric railways traversing the southern part of the province at the turn of the century also reached Niagara about this time.

Niagara-on-the-Lake saw an influx of visitors and their families who came to stay for long vacations in the summer. Old houses were enlarged to accommodate parents, children, relations, friends, and servants. New summer residences were built, great frame houses with high ceilinged rooms, verandahs festooned with gingerbread, roofs with turrets and widow's walks. A religious camp ground grew up at Chatauqua on the western side of the town. A new era of relative prosperity was born and, at least in the summer, the people of Niagara could bask in a little more than the sun. It was perhaps an age of leisure, destined to preserve rather than destroy the community as a whole. New hotels, like the Queen's Royal

on the waterfront, were built, but mainly for the old-fashioned summer vacation before the days of touring by automobile. The resort era lasted until world war I and was at its height at the turn of the century when a prospectus of the town shows some of the joys of the place at that time. In the 1920s and 1930s Niagara-on-the-Lake was still on the steamer route but the car was taking its toll of the old summer trade; once again Niagara retired, to become a haven for its citizens and a few who respected its peace. The dock company had folded, the old industries had disappeared. Fruit and vegetable canning came briefly, but there was not much development otherwise. The town was almost asleep to the casual observer but, as in all such places, its social heart was still beating hard.

During the late 1930s, towards the end of the Depression, the provincial government undertook the reconstruction of Fort George. Much had disappeared into the ground in the intervening century and extensive archaeology, and research by Ronald L. Way, formed the bases for this work. Fort Mississauga still awaits attention.

The boom following world war II has affected Niagara-on-the-Lake too, and greater and easier travel has seen more people enjoy it and consider making their home there. Still secluded, it catered as a dormitory to nearby cities, and at the same time has attracted to itself special industries not the least of which is boat-building. The pressures of change are here once again, the constant erosion of early building always threatening, through either sheer destruction or disastrous mutilation. So far the balance has been maintained, with more people engaging in the preservation of early structures and their sympathetic adaptation than ever before. The fight goes on, mostly privately, in recognition of the town's unique quality and despite the lack of public support to encourage the right attitudes and responses to the task. For even in centennial year two early buildings disappeared for lack

of public imagination and co-operation with private interest. Nevertheless the balance is always redressed. Particular mention should be made of one or two, and their successors who have added in recent times more than most people generally know: the late Mrs Kathleen Drope whose work is both evident and unrevealed, the late Carl Banke, master-carpenter and joiner whose hand was sure and sympathetic, and firms like Slade and Bezuyen that follow suit.

So we inherit a community whose foundation was laid before 1800, that spans the history of this part of Canada, and illustrates better than all the major cities of Ontario combined what early nineteenth century Upper Canada was like. In order to appreciate that, however, it is necessary to recognize the earlier examples from the later insertions and a brief résumé of their characteristics seems appropriate.

On Queen street, the principal shopping area, the building may appear to be a little haphazard especially compared with the regular and formal treatment of Walton street in Port Hope, Ontario. But it pre-dates the speculative building boom of the latter, and stretches over a longer period. To all intents and purposes Queen represents the 'primitive' stage of main street development, the initial phase where every man builds for himself regardless of his neighbour. The essential difference from the current approach is that discipline reigned – in the simple elements used in the design, the restricted list of materials available, the repetition of distinctive features like windows, cornices, and shopfronts, generally good proportions arising from the functional relation between floor space and storey height and the traditional building shapes of the period. The result generally was harmony, even in sign lettering and symbols; need one say more?

In the residential parts of the town you will find most of the older houses built close to the street, so close in fact that a new survey of the

town in 1909 found that some actually encroached upon the street allowance! This still allows sixty-six feet or one chain more or less between buildings at the minimum, a generous enough space in a small town. Later builders, setting newer houses in between, have usually subscribed to the more recent preference for a front garden and so the buildings are set back; now regulation encourages this. The result is visually rather remarkable, for the town's streets become an irregular pattern of contracting and expanding street spaces, fascinating to behold and always rewarding to walk through. With the accompanying fences, hedges, and gardens, the town of Niagara-on-the-Lake is a particular pleasure in spring, summer, and fall, and in winter it also has its charm.

Mention should be made of the more common dwelling types with reference to layout or plan, and shape or form. The almost infinite variations require constant reference to the 'typical,' here described for the deviation to

The south side of Queen street, between Regent and King, c1870. The Court House with its cupola is in the centre. Alma's Store, on the right of the picture, shows clearly the original arcaded detail and the traditional T; it was altered c1875 to match the brick building erected next to it. The Sherlock block shows to the right of the Court House, and the Sign of the Pineapple is second to the left.

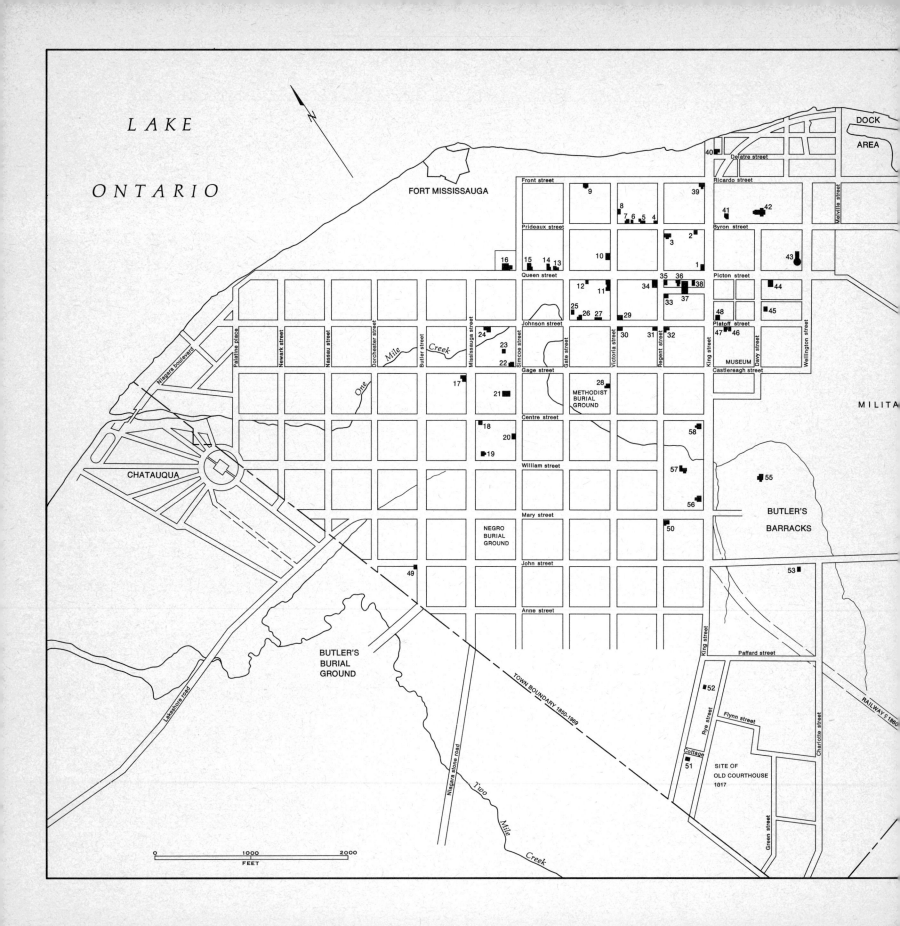

LAKE

ONTARIO

DOCK
AREA

FORT MISSISSAUGA

Front street
40
Delatre street
Ricardo street
Melville street

9
39
8
41   42
7 6 5 4
Byron street
Prideaux street
2
3
43
16
15 14 13
1
Queen street
Picton street
35 36
12   11   34   38   44
25   33   37
26 27   29
48   45
Johnson street
30 31 32
47 46
24
23
Gate street   Victoria street   Regent street
King street   MUSEUM
Simcoe street   Castlereagh street   Davy street   Wellington street
22
Gage street
17
28   MILITA
21   METHODIST
BURIAL
GROUND
18   58
Centre street
20
19
57   55
BUTLER'S
William street   BARRACKS
56
Mary street
NEGRO
BURIAL   50
GROUND   John street   53

CHATAUQUA

Niagara boulevard
Palatine place
Newark street
Nassau street
Dorchester street
One
Mile
Butler's
Creek
Mississauga street

49   Anne street

King street   Paffard street

BUTLER'S
BURIAL
GROUND   TOWN BOUNDARY 1850-1969   RAILWAY c 1860

52
Rye street   Flynn street   Charlotte street   Green street

Lakeshore road
Niagara stone road   Two
Mile
Creek   Cottage
51   SITE OF
OLD COURTHOUSE
1017

0   1000   2000
FEET

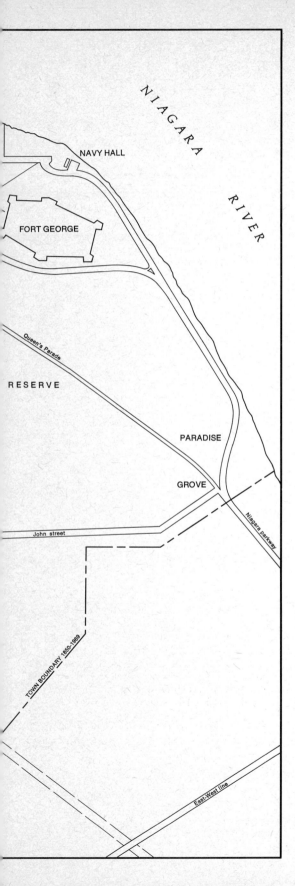

NIAGARA RIVER

NAVY HALL

FORT GEORGE

Queen's Parade

RESERVE

PARADISE

GROVE

Niagara parkway

John street

TOWN BOUNDARY 1850-1969

East-West line

Plan of Niagara 1970
The locations of all the buildings in the three
tours are indicated by their numbers.

be understood. In layout the formal arrangement resulted in a regular ground floor plan of centre hall with reception rooms to either side facing the street and usually small bedrooms or slip rooms behind. The upper storey was reserved for sleeping space mainly. The kitchen might be in one of several places: in the basement as in a town house, in a wing to the rear or occasionally to the side, or in a back corner of the main block. The number of openings or 'bays' with the typical centre hall plan might be from three to five across the front of the building; more would be unusual.

Two shapes or forms occur most frequently, the first with a roof sloped to front and back with gable ends, or the side walls built up to meet it, and with end chimneys. This is, perhaps, the most common form of the early house throughout the province. The second, and particularly popular in Niagara, is the hipped roof sometimes referred to as the 'cottage' roof, sloped on all four sides of the building and associated with inside chimneys or stacks placed within the body of the house. In Todmorden Mills, now buried in the sprawl of Toronto, there is a small house of just such form ascribed to Parshall Terry, a former citizen of Niagara, who moved to the new capital in 1798 and was drowned in the Don River in 1808. Later examples with this basic shape are familiarly known as the Ontario Cottage.

What follows in this book is but an introduction to Niagara-on-the-Lake: you may wish yourself to explore it further. Go on foot, if a horse and carriage cannot be obtained; take it, if your stride has not recovered, in easy stages. Glance along every street, sense its appeal, and follow your gaze, pausing wherever and whenever necessary to look at an early building, taking in all that you see, from the total view to every particular. This heritage still stands for you to enjoy, in old Niagara-on-the-Lake, a phoenix surviving.

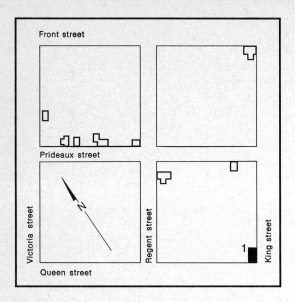

One of the oldest continuing pharmacies in the country, and certainly the oldest in Upper Canada (to become, after Confederation, the province of Ontario), Field's Drug Store is to be restored as the Niagara Apothecary. The present building was enlarged and renovated from an earlier structure in 1866 when Henry Paffard moved the business to this address. (Paffard was several times mayor of Niagara and saw to the planting of many of the street trees, now in their maturity.) In the early history of the pharmacy advertisements referred to its location at the sign of the Golden Mortar, the traditional symbol for an apothecary, frequently used as a decorative hanging sign to identify its position. Many early account books, prescription books, and most of the containers of the old business have been recovered and are on display.

Earlier, possibly from 1834, the building served as the office of E.C. Campbell, barrister, who became eventually a judge of the county court. Its previous smaller size is corroborated by changes in structure at the back and the curious foundation in the larger and older section to the front which is faced with limestone foreign to the area and similar to that from Kingston. Such stone may well have been ballast in a lake schooner.

Outside, the decorated front is representative of mid-Victorian store design using larger glass panes more readily available at the time and more appropriate for the purpose of display. The Florentine windows with the arcaded design and roundel above are typical of the Italianate style of the 1860s and 1870s; and the delicate twisted colonettes with their elaborate capitals and 'drops' or pendants on brackets supporting the cornice above are all part of the architectural fashion of the time.

The interior is substantially that of the 1866 renovations with heavy, ornate counters and shelves, and cabinets lining the wall, the titles on the tiers of drawers on the east side indicating their former contents. The prescription counter at the back is part of an old arrangement too. At the ceiling the broad, deeply moulded cornice is typical of the period, while the bold and intricate medallions, so involved and undercut in their florid design of basket-weave and interwoven fruit and flowers, are somewhat reminiscent of Dresden china. From each medallion hung a crystal gasolier, all of which are still in the Niagara area, but in private hands. Evidence of gas piping does survive but it must have been arranged for a private plant which was a fairly common device in the mid-nineteenth century.

The Ontario College of Pharmacy undertook the restoration with the help of the Ontario Heritage Foundation and the federal government. The Niagara Foundation, pledged to the preservation of the local heritage, saved this building for posterity by purchasing it after the last owner, Mr E.W. Field, descendant of one of the Loyalist families which settled Niagara, retired in 1964 and died in 1965, leaving no one to carry on the business.

1

The Niagara Apothecary

1820

Queen street

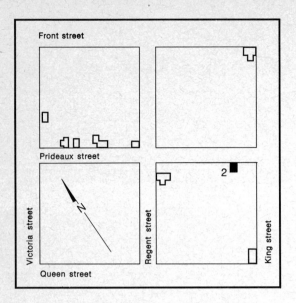

Typical of the smaller frame dwellings of old Niagara-on-the-Lake, the McKee House reflects many of the local characteristics in its position and the elements of its design. This small house placed close to the street like most early buildings exhibits, however, far more of its original detail on the exterior, including the sash of small glass in a common arrangement of twelve over eight panes. Here the door is placed at the side of the house in an asymmetrical elevation, with the gable end to the front.

Half hidden by overshadowing trees the house escaped being plotted by recent aerial surveys: its seclusion is entire in the midst of Niagara!

The interior is simple but representative of the smaller house of the day. Fireplaces appear to have gone or to have been absent, their stove counterpart serving as the original system of heating.

A deed poll, dated 19 April 1823, made by Thomas Powis refers to this property, and its terms are rather a delight to read. 'In consideration of the natural love and affection which he had and bore,' his granddaughters, his daughter, and son-in-law, one Alexander McKee, schoolmaster, in return for part of Lot 34, were bound and obliged 'to support and maintain the said Thomas Powis during his natural life and to find and provide for him good sufficient and comfortable clothes board washing makeing and mending and to furnish him with a room to himself and sufficient wood and candle light and to discharge any debts that he might then owe and procure him medical aid when necessary ...' Curiously no transaction is recorded between Thomas Powis and Andrew Heron, who was granted the property by the Crown before the War.

2

McKee-Dodson House

CIRCA 1835

18 Prideaux street

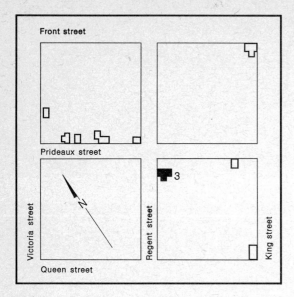

Jemima Stewart, mother of Alexander Stewart, is known to have purchased the property from Augustus Jones in 1818, but a mortgage to Alexander Stewart, the elder, also refers to this lot in 1800 and his widow made a war losses claim for a house in the amount of £500.

This house, named after its first inhabitant and probable builder, the young lawyer, Alexander Stewart, is one of the designs in arcaded brick which rose in the greater building period a quarter of a century or so from the end of the War. Elsewhere in the Niagara frontier settlements (for example, in Lewiston), similar arcading survives. The detail is a familiar one in Regency houses, much favoured by John Nash and his contemporaries, and occurs frequently in town houses and terraces of the time. Here, in the Stewart House, the device is somewhat simplified without the arcading in the lower storey which occurs in the MacDougal-Harrison House (14) on Queen street.

The relatively simple exterior belies the glory within – a magnificent and elegant sweeping stair, semi-elliptical in plan rising behind a decorative archway from the back of the hall: a lady dressed in the fashion of the period is the only adornment that befits it. However, the house is a curious flush, almost suggesting a show of finery to impress, for it is only one room deep, with fireplaces against the back wall. Similar arrangements do occur locally combined with kitchen ells. The dining room to the left is intact, but the drawing room to the right is now altered. The kitchen, originally in the basement with its cooking hearth, for later convenience was housed in a more recent rear wing. Upstairs, the largest bedroom with fireplace and alcoves probably served also as the private withdrawing room of the house.

3

Stewart-McLeod House

CIRCA 1830

42 Prideaux street

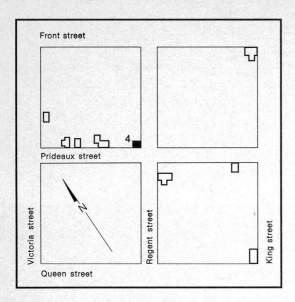

In 1796 Elizabeth Thompson was granted Lot 28, and in 1823 her holding was forfeited as a result of indebtedness. John Breaken-ridge, barrister, purchased it for a modest sum and sold it to David Botsford in 1826. The property then went through the hands of two officers of the Niagara Harbour and Dock Company, Philip Delatre in 1832 and Robert Melville in 1843. In 1846 Richard Howard, innkeeper, and former proprietor of the Angel Inn (33) on Market street, obtained the building and, according to Janet Carnochan in the *History of Niagara*, his new stand was known as the Promenade House.

No doubt one of the establishments referred to rather caustically by Mrs Jameson in her comments on the apparent dissolute beha-viour of the citizens, the Promenade House must in the early days have served quite a clientele. Its presence in the midst of the com-munity suggests a greater tolerance than modern attitudes, but life at the time appears to have been a very curious opposite of rough-ness and elegance, and the people were cap-able, possibly, of accepting or assuming a matching colour: a freedom no doubt con-sidered somewhat debauched by a lady of propriety and intelligence, like mixing salt herring with poached salmon.

With its elegant small brick front, in the decorative Flemish bond, a transom light decorated with Regency filigree, and cames ornamented with lead rosettes, the building hardly seems commodious enough for an hotel. But out behind stretched a long frame wing which housed other rooms, probably further sleeping quarters, kitchen and domes-tic arrangements. A stable also must have stood on the grounds.

What remains, however, is still elegant testi-mony to the hostelries of old Niagara. The interior has fine trim, and mantelpieces. Preservation is underway as some of the sash at the back indicate, but eaves and front door need restoring.

4

The Promenade House

CIRCA 1820

55 Prideaux street

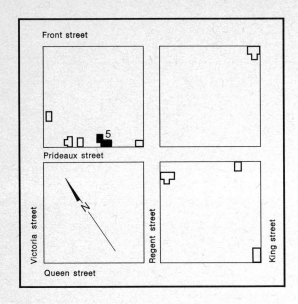

A description of a house with wings existing on this site and destroyed during the Fire of 10 December 1813 occurs in a war losses claim made out by Dr Robert Kerr, physician and surgeon to the Indian Department, who was one of Niagara's most respected citizens. Old foundations found under the present building may belong to the original: it is not known how much was rebuilt on earlier walls.

Kerr had been recommended in 1790 by Lord Dorchester, governor of Canada, for a seat on the Executive Council of the intended province of Upper Canada. The appointment did not come through but he became a magistrate of the surrogate court. Later in the 1790s he was grand master of the Grand Masonic Lodge of Upper Canada. In 1822 he moved to Albany, New York, where he died in 1824. His wife, who died in 1794, was a daughter of Mollie Brant and Sir William Johnson.

Again, the house is built on the street, with its long garden stretching down to Front with a view to the lake: a place for garden, vegetable plot, and a cow. The brick front with the decorative Flemish bond has a simple entrance with fan contained within a rectangular transom. Fenestration, however, is irregular, the hall placed off-centre, but with the principal rooms on each side of it. The mark of another doorway at the centre window of the group to the right of the front door suggests some provision for a surgery or separate office entrance, and internal refurbishing of this large room may also indicate some alteration of the plan. The side extension, although later, follows the detail of the original on the outside; internally it was up-to-date.

The interior still retains much of the original fine detail of the early nineteenth century with its delicate mouldings, intricately worked mantelpieces, and a second-floor drawing room with a fireplace flanked by alcoves.

5

Kerr-Wooll House

CIRCA 1815 *Demeath*

69 Prideaux street

Front street

Prideaux street

Victoria street

Regent street

Queen street

King street

6

Typical of the smaller houses of Niagara and like other early buildings, placed close to the street, 83 and 87 Prideaux street are neighbours of the Kerr-Wooll House (5) with only one later house (c1910) set back between them. The arrangement illustrates better than any other the juxtaposition of large and small residences, presumably indicating relative wealth, in a community built when respectful co-existence was practised. The example survives as a reminder, to present-day developers and planners, of the model of a community which is self-perpetuating providing its people respect it for its quality.

One of the houses, and probably 83, the Dobie-Campbell House, was owned by John Davidson, the joiner and carpenter who provided, we now believe, so much of the fine woodwork in Niagara between the late 1820s and early 1860s. Davidson is certainly credited with the pulpitum in St Andrew's, in 1840, and as being one of the Davidsons who helped build St Vincent de Paul in 1834, and whose brother was killed in falling off the tower. John Davidson was noted as a builder of exquisite curved staircases, and, according to one of his descendants, in the mid-nineteenth century his reputation earned him a job in Cleveland, Ohio, where he was entrusted with such complicated structures after a single demonstration of his ability. We now wonder how many beautiful staircases he did construct in Niagara, for the elliptical sweep in the Stewart House (3) is certainly a masterpiece. History has it that Davidson's employment in St Mark's came in for criticism in the early 1840s, presumably at the time of the chancel and transept additions, for he was not a parishioner: could the accomplished staircase in the Rectory some fifteen years later be the result of a renewal of faith in the work of such a superior artisan?

In 1833 Matthew Dobie, blacksmith, purchased Lot 26, on which 83 and 87 Prideaux street stand, selling it to John Davidson in 1839 with an increase in value suggesting

some improvement: probably this indicates the building of the Dobie-Campbell House.

The Dobie House is a typical small dwelling of a storey and a half with end gables, a structure of timber frame sheathed in clapboard, and a three-bay front. Again the layout is the common centre hall plan with later additions. Detail on the outside and inside is simple, although later improvements obscure the original.

6

Dobie-Campbell House

CIRCA 1835

83 Prideaux street

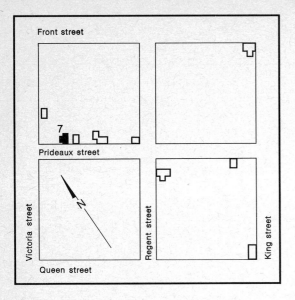

Whereas its neighbour, the Dobie-Campbell House, appears to be an earlier structure, this building is probably John Davidson's creation.

This house is also built right on the front of the lot, but with its gable facing the street, resulting in a side hall layout. However, it is similar in proportion to the adjoining house. Later additions of a side ell, and consequent embellishments of a simple bargeboard, pendants or drops, and finials, suggest mid or later Victorian improvements by a subsequent owner, possibly John Torrance (or Terrance), c1860, or John Marchbands Lawder in the later 1860s.

The lacework frill about the eaves and other ornament are slight concessions to the Gothic Revival in an attempt perhaps to create a cottage ornée. The curious louvred vestibule, like that of 83, is somehow reminiscent of a sedan chair and is probably a later Victorian improvement.

7

Davidson-Campbell House

CIRCA 1845

87 Prideaux street

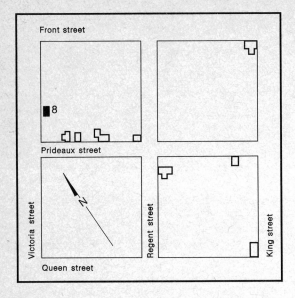

Front street

Prideaux street

Victoria street

Regent street

King street

Queen street

William Kirby apparently lived here in the 1850s for his son John was born in the house in 1854. The story persists that an army captain has always lived here, and that it may have been built by an officer who had served in Butler's Rangers or in the local garrison.

The original owner of the building was apparently Samuel Winterbottom, resident of Niagara during the War. By a will dated 1840 he left the house to his son, William Bowers Winterbottom, who had been called to the Bar in 1830 and at his death sixty-five years later was the oldest bencher in the province. Curiously no earlier transaction is recorded aside from the granting of the lot to William Cain in 1796.

This small storey-and-a-quarter frame house demonstrates the joy and delight that an early building can become to serve this day and age. The exterior is basically a five-bay cottage, and belongs to the complement of smaller houses that fill out the town's older residential quarter.

The interior is simply finished, the trim in the manner of the period, and with certain adaptations to later preferences.

8

Winterbottom-Gullion House

CIRCA 1835

134 Victoria street

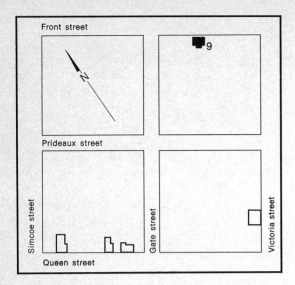

Front street

Prideaux street

Simcoe street

Gate street

Victoria street

Queen street

9

This was the home from 1855 until his death in 1906 of William Kirby, author of the *Annals of Niagara*, *The Golden Dog*, *Canadian Idylls*, and other works, as the plaque outside describes. Typical of the average house in the quarter-century of building after the fire, the exterior of the main part is only slightly modified from its former distinction. The interior, however, has been more drastically treated and less survives than one would expect from the outside.

The doorway is a notable feature of the house, and a design typical of the town for the period prior to 1830, variations of which occur elsewhere. Probably the French windows are an alteration contributed by Kirby to follow the style of the mid nineteenth century verandah which has since disappeared. The roughcast finish, a form of stucco rendering, is a common replacement of earlier clapboard. Upper sash, cornice, and eaves returns, however, survive while other details like the chimneys have been modified in the course of repairs during the years.

On the interior, the familiar centre hall layout is followed, with principal rooms on either side and, originally, smaller rooms behind. End chimneys with fireplaces provided early heating: one elegant mantelpiece of the immediate post-War period still graces the parlour.

9

Kirby House

CIRCA 1818

130 Front street

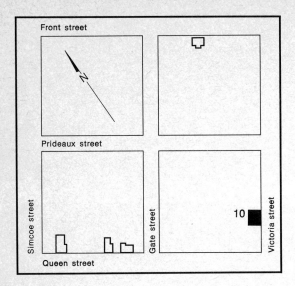

The building was constructed by John Wilson, son of 'Irish John,' keeper of the hotel where the Law Society of Upper Canada first met (see 12).

Again, this early house is placed close to the street line. Here the common, clapboarded frame, a storey and a half in gable form, is rather shallow from front to back with a lean-to addition across the rear. The house is a five-bay front with simple centre doorcase ornamented by a plain transom light.

The original internal arrangement appears to have been similar to the Miller House (50) at Mary and Regent, with a large room serving the family – a keeping room with a large cooking fireplace to the right or north end. The centre hall contains the stair rising to a landing and returning toward the front of the house. The parlour was undoubtedly to the left and may have been stove-heated with a bedroom behind. Upstairs there was the characteristic subdivision for sleeping space. The wing behind may have been for greater space or the later accommodation of more convenient cooking facilities.

The trim where it has survived is the finely scaled type of the immediate post-War years. The staircase with its ascending dado rail is uncommon in Niagara and seldom occurs later on: the next decorative treatment of such spaces is the late Victorian mode of dado panelling or embossed paper finish.

10

Wilson-Kent House

CIRCA 1816

175 Victoria street

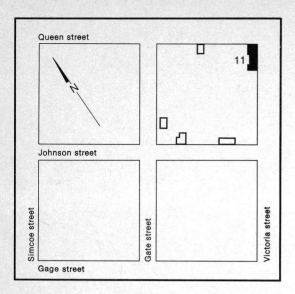

Queen street

Johnson street

Simcoe street

Gage street

Gate street

Victoria street

11

At the corner of Queen and Victoria is Mc-Clelland's, in business for over a century and a half – since the War in fact – which is no mean record. It is still the delight of the townspeople and visitors alike whose custom is greeted by the courtesy such an establishment bestows, especially if the many delicacies the store contains are sought. Cheese is a specialty, besides many other exotic items which share the shelves with everyday needs. The great T sign is the traditional one of the provisioner, similar to that which once belonged to Alma's Store (35).

The property, however, has had previous owners, including the merchant, Lewis Clement, who advertised in the *Gleaner* in the late 1820s, and was given a large mortgage in 1834. McClelland's purchased the property in 1873.

The upper storey of McClelland's has lost only window sash, but stone quoins to the brickwork and the ornamental fan in the gable are early details; the shopfront is a more modern plate-glass 'improvement.' In the rear wing there exists a large windlass for hauling goods into the upper floor for storage, a relic of the days when infrequent deliveries by boat required the merchant to buy his stock in barrel, cask, and crate. The adjoining extension on Queen street is later, believed to be a structure of the 1880s.

11

McClelland's West End Store
CIRCA 1835

106 Queen street

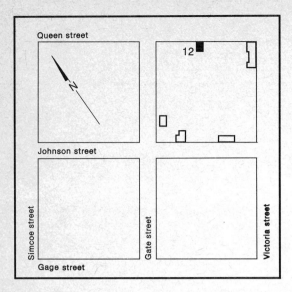

The rest of this block, apart from the more modern, and incidentally less sympathetic, intrusions, is one of considerable architectural interest still, if allowance is made for the erosion of significant detail in some buildings. At the far end of the block, at the corner of Gate, a plaque marks the site of Wilson's Hotel, scene of the founding of the Law Society of Upper Canada in 1797.

126 Queen Street is shown in all its glory in a measured drawing of 1926 made under the guidance of Professor Eric R. Arthur, who recognized the specialty of the early building of Upper Canada. With its original sashing and doorway restored and a coat of arms emblazoned above, it could certainly pass as a Regency front. The date appears to be *c*1825. At one time it is said to have served as a Customs House, where William Kirby was the collector.

122 and 124 Queen, next door to the east, form a charming range of mid nineteenth century dwellings with large windows below doubling as small stores. This, the Evans Block, still retains most of its original finish and detail on the exterior.

Nearby, at 118 Queen, is the Gollop House, the front stoop decorated by the blacksmith who once lived there. The doorcase is noteworthy, and a good example from the 1820s, the ornamental pilasters and high head board above reminding one of designs for mantelpieces. The chimneys to the house suggest fireplaces. The front, with door flanked by a window on either side indicates a typical centre hall plan. The earlier finish would have been clapboard which, with small paned sash and shutters, completes the authentic picture.

12

The Customs House

CIRCA 1825

126 Queen street

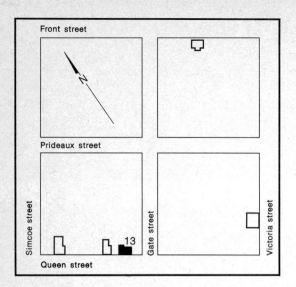

Extensive personal accounts of 1823 kept by Mrs Agnes Rogers who had an hotel here suggest a building or rebuilding at this date. This house, like the Kerr-Wooll House (5), is an asymmetrical front, yet still formal in its fenestration. The arrangement provides a large room, the drawing room, to the left of the hall and a corresponding large bedroom or upper drawing room above. The room to the right has an arched recess at the back suggesting a space for a sideboard, a common dining room arrangement. Much of the exterior has retained its early detail, the doorcase with its sidelights and fanlight being noteworthy and the early sash typical. The present finish of stucco lined to imitate cut stone may be a mid or later nineteenth century covering to replace the earlier (and harder to maintain) clapboard. The house is a frame structure and has suffered minor changes and additions and the loss of an old rear wing.

Inside, the detail is representative of the finer and more pretentious houses of the town, the Rogers having been one of the earliest families to live there. A fine staircase, trim of delicate profile, and elaborate mantelpieces, including one of curiously almost Baroque Germanic convolution, and one fireplace with alcoves arched at the top beside it decorate the house.

A sketch exists of the Rogers block which was built in 1833 at the corner of Victoria next to this house, but long since demolished. This appeared to have been built for commercial purposes, and the illustration shows a handsome brick front, with stone sills and lintels to windows, three storeys high, eminently suited to such a position.

13

Rogers-Harrison House

CIRCA 1823

157 Queen street

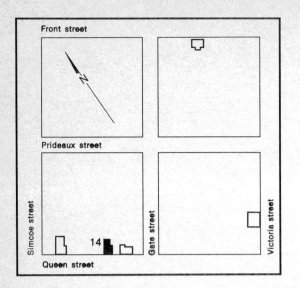

The most important owner, after whom the house is now named, was Colonel Daniel MacDougal, born in Scotland in 1782, coming to Canada in 1786, and taking part in the War at Ogdensburgh and Lundy's Lane, where he was severely wounded and lay on the battlefield all night, to recover and live in this house from 1849 until his death in 1866. A Roman Catholic, Colonel MacDougal was a great supporter of the Church of St Vincent de Paul. For many years he held the position of treasurer to the united counties of Lincoln, Welland, and Haldimand.

This house pre-dates Colonel MacDougal's tenure by some years, for the lot was in the Clench name from 1811 to 1820 when it was sold to Adam Crysler, who was probably the builder.

Always associated with Niagara-on-the-Lake, this excellent and charming example of a town house with its crow-stepped gables and end chimneys and distinctive brick front of double arcades is perhaps the best surviving example of this design. It seems as though it had been intended not as an isolated house but as part of a range of similar fronts, expecting its neighbours to nestle up to it, but the terrace never materialized.

The sashes of the windows are original. The doorcase with its six-panel door, intricate sidelights, and elliptical transom filled with complicated tracery of cames and ornamental rosettes is almost too elaborate: that it has survived is almost a miracle and speaks well of the owners who cherished it.

Inside, the plan is another type common in Niagara where a side hall with stair adjoins double parlours alongside, or a front or best parlour with fireplace and alcoves and a rear or dining parlour similarly heated by a fireplace. The rear wing contains domestic offices and more bedroom space, but the kitchen was originally behind the stair. Upstairs the plan follows a similar layout, with three rooms serving as bedrooms having fireplaces, two with mantelpieces of elaborate design, with a fourth room over the front door. The mantelpieces are like that noted in the Rogers-Harrison House (13) next door, a very odd and overly elaborate design with colonettes of attenuated hour-glass form, distinctly Germanic and Baroque in inspiration, a prototype of which has been seen in southern New York state and another is said to exist near Utica in upstate New York. Trim, generally, is finely scaled, indicative of an early date, with symmetrical profiles heralding a preference of the later 1820s and early 1830s.

14

MacDougal-Harrison House

CIRCA 1820

165 Queen street

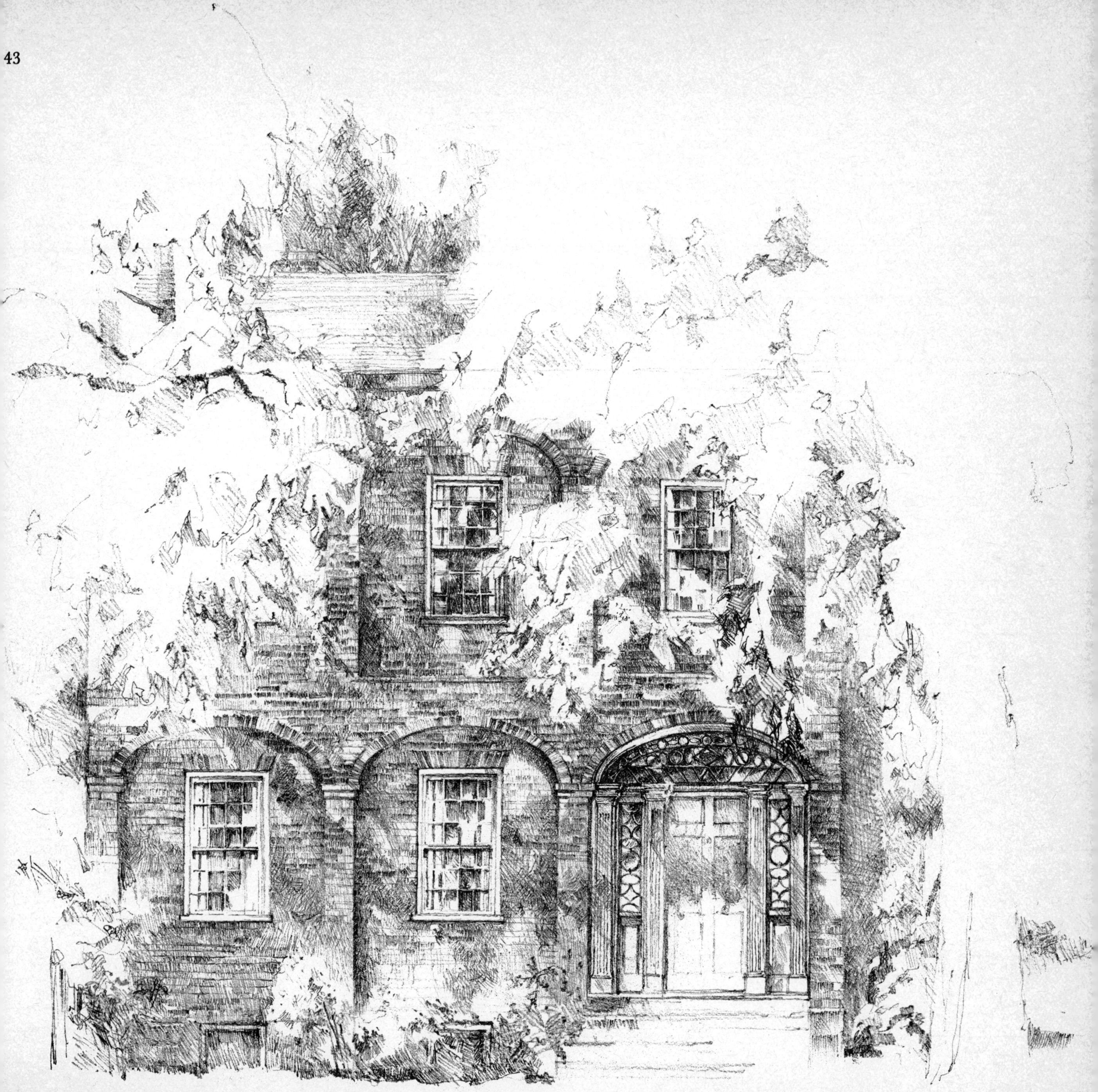

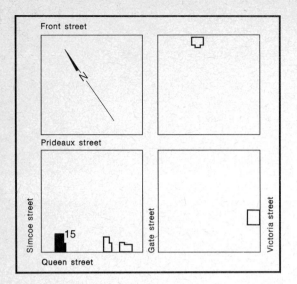

'Cottage' is rather a misnomer for this quite substantial dwelling built by a wealthy merchant of the town, the provisioner, Ralph Morden Crysler, related to the other family of the same name which settled beside the Upper St Lawrence. The house is believed to have been built in 1822 and, when Mr Crysler's fortunes failed in the late 1830s, was sold. Then it came into the hands of Lawyer Hall (Charles L. Hall) who, in the late 1840s, probably made the Greek Revival improvements and modified the plan slightly.

The house is a three-bay design in wood, a full two storeys in height with a very low pitched roof, hipped in form, and four end chimneys.

To preserve the symmetry, one chimney, that over the hall, appears to be a dummy for it has no fireplaces attached, but it may have had a stove using it. The exterior is one of several noteworthy examples of the carpenter's and joiner's skill in its elaborate cornice ornamented with modillions, carefully worked pilaster treatment, and carved Ionic caps, a design comparable to the Breakenridge-Hawley House (19) on Mississauga and the Clench House (24) on Johnson, of approximately the same date.

The entrance, a very handsome essay in the Greek mode, is now on the side and opens into a stair hall. A front drawing room and rear dining room are in the main block with a small room behind the hall. The kitchen is a large room in the rear wing with a cooking fireplace at the end, and originally servants' rooms above. Upstairs in the main block is a magnificent suite of bedrooms, an archway with folding doors between, and matching mantelpieces, very elaborate, and with pilasters of the curious elongated hour-glass shape noted elsewhere in the town. This room could obviously serve as an upper drawing room or perhaps as a small ballroom.

Side door and porch, and changes to the hall including the stair, appear to replace an entrance directly from the street, their design mid nineteenth century and likely by Lawyer Hall. The verandahs to the rear wing were built about the turn of the century and are similar to the additions to the Richardson-Kiely House (16) nearby.

There is a great 'seahorse' newel similar to the slighter example in the Brook House *c*1850 (28) on Victoria street; the winding stair with its heavy balustrade of vase-shaped turnings resembles that in the Rectory of 1858 (41). The downstairs drawing room has a marble mantelpiece of the 1840s or 1850s, the plain pilastered design seen in the Richardson-Kiely House (16) and slightly more delicate than those in the Court House (37) of 1847.

15

Crysler-Rigg House
CIRCA 1822 *Roslyn Cottage*

187 Queen street

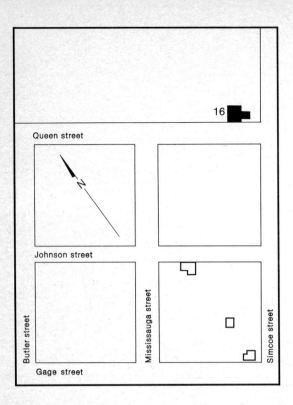

This house, constructed by Charles Richardson, a barrister, and member of parliament for Niagara from 1832 to 1834, is situated on property once owned by Lockhart who built the house at the north-west corner of Simcoe and Gage, now known as Storrington (22). As with many older houses in the town, it was enlarged around the turn of the century, during the resort era, and was festooned with galleries for summer enjoyment.

The nucleus of the house is still easily recognized with its centre doorway, adorned with sidelights and a generous fanlight, flanked by two windows on each side and a Palladian window centred above with similar fenestration. The shape is a hip roof with end chimneys.

In layout the house is the conventional centre hall with the principal rooms to either side, those to the left forming a double drawing room connected by an archway and with similar mantelpieces of walnut now disguised discreetly by white paint. To the right is the dining room, with a simple marble mantel of pilastered design, rather similar to others of the late 1840s or 1850s. Behind this room is the old kitchen with its great cooking fireplace and built-in cooker or sheet-iron oven with firebox below, a device very similar to one designed by Count Rumford, the late eighteenth century authority and pioneer in heating design. Below stairs is a roomy basement with indications of another fireplace, probably an auxiliary cooking hearth in what must have served as a still room. A strange vaulted chamber leads off the cellar to the north and legend has it that this was an underground passage to Fort Mississauga although it would have been an excellent cold store or root cellar too.

Upstairs the familiar plan is repeated, with large bedrooms and wide hall to the Palladian window. Interior detail is in good order with wood trim of the pilastered sort with corner blocks in important rooms and simple mitred forms elsewhere, and plaster cornices and rosettes to ceilings. The staircase is a fine example with walnut handrail, tapered balusters, and a scroll supported by a baluster cage enclosing a turned brass newel. Halfway up at the turn of the stair is a curved door and doorcase, an accomplished piece of joinery.

4

16

Richardson-Kiely House

1832

209 Queen street

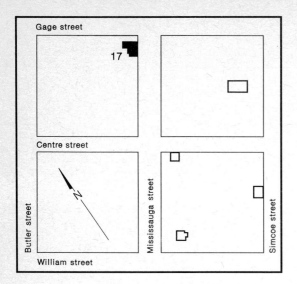

The one-acre lot, number 159 in the town plot, was granted by the crown in 1816 to John D. Servos, of a United Empire Loyalist family. In 1818 he sold to Garry Camp, who a few months later obtained a mortgage from the merchants Robert and Peter McDougall of York, selling the property to them in the fall of the same year for twice the sum, which suggests that the lot had been improved by a house. According to Janet Carnochan, this was at one time a well-known private school, Dr Whitelaw's, one of many such institutions which provided tutoring to local families.

This is a rather unusual building, with the main block served by a chimney near the middle of the house and a long ell off one side facing the other street. The front is asymmetrical now, following the layout within, which may have been changed.

The centre chimney had a cooking hearth and bakeoven in the basement, and fireplaces back-to-back above. The plan has a foreshortened hall with stairs against the front wall, the major rooms grouped around it. Behind this is the ell, believed to be an addition for the school function, possibly providing for a schoolroom below and dormitory above.

Detail is simple, with the typical finely scaled mouldings of immediate post-War period in the main front section, and simpler profiles in the ell extension.

17

Camp-Thompson House

1818

307 Mississauga street

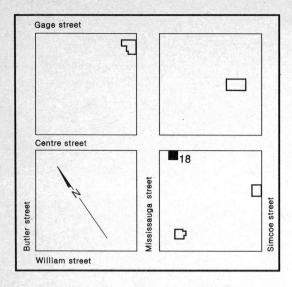

The original owner of the house was John Breakenridge, barrister, who died in 1828, leaving it to his widow who held a school there in the 1830s.

This two-storey brick house with hipped roof and end chimneys may be compared with its later counterpart, the Post House (29) at Johnson and Victoria; the arrangement of the façades is somewhat similar although the details differ. The house is part of a trio once in the Breakenridge name, and the last to be built, the Hawley House (19) at Mississauga and William streets being the intermediate, and the core of the Creen House (20) on Simcoe being the first, all three in the same four-acre block.

The exterior is plain, relying solely on its good proportions and soft pink, hand-made brick for its pleasing effect. The brickwork is in common bond on the street fronts, with projecting string courses to demarcate the storeys. Windows are relatively small, and still with their original sash. Little fuss is given to the doorcase in contrast to its predecessor on the next corner, the simple rectangular opening here perhaps being a concession to simplicity to fit the strong horizontality of the string course and create a substantial appearance, four-square and permanent. The doorway with sidelights and transom is one of the plainest in Niagara.

Because of the elevation of the ground floor, the basement kitchen, with its cooking fireplace and bake-oven, is high and airy. Again, this typical centre hall plan has the principal rooms to the front, smaller rooms behind, a pattern which is repeated on the second floor. The house originally was heated entirely by fireplaces, there being four to a floor plus that in the basement.

The trim is the delicately scaled variety of the 1820s, mitred at corners and including architraves, chair rails, baseboards, and a variety of mantelpiece designs on the pilaster and centre panel theme. However, as might be expected, the staircase is a simple scheme, a straight flight with tapered round balusters, oval rail, and slender tapered square newels.

18

Breakenridge-Ure House

CIRCA 1823

240 Centre street

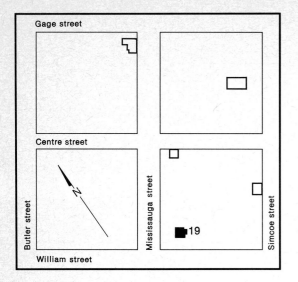

John Breakenridge, the first owner of the building, was noted in his obituary in 1828 for having built 'several of the most elegant and tasty houses in town ...'

Perhaps the most resplendent doorway in Niagara graces this frame house, a much embroidered design bringing to mind those of the Federal period in New England. The builder of the house did not finish there, but pulled all the stops to employ that marvellous material, the native white pine, to decorate his exterior with fluted pilasters, crowned by Ionic capitals, with florid ramshorns and a modillion cornice carried along the eaves as a gutter and across the gable ends in a pediment feature. Some years ago, before the present owner started preservation of the house and the restoration of some of its essential features, the drabness of the exterior and neglected appearance concealed this magnificence.

The interior layout is a typical centre hall plan with ell extension. The kitchen was discovered to have been in the rear wing and a cooking fireplace and bakeoven have been reconstructed there. Elsewhere great pains were taken to copy remaining detail over several years to bring the house back into condition and care was taken to preserve many of the essential interior details. The old French windows made by cutting the sashed openings to the floor strongly suggest a concession to the verandah afterwards attached to the house: in recent preservation work this later feature was modified.

The dining room with its alcove with flanking cupboards is a noteworthy and original feature. The archway framing this alcove has a semi-elliptical shape supported on gently convex pilasters reeded spirally, a very complicated piece of joinery. Original mantelpieces survive and with the trim are composed of the delicate profiles associated with the decade after the War.

The coach-house behind was part of the preservation scheme, a conversion from an older building, and complements the layout. The house stands on one of the one-acre lots forming the original subdivision of the town but, in contrast to most early buildings, is set back from front and side streets.

19

Breakenridge-Hawley House

CIRCA 1818

392 Mississauga street

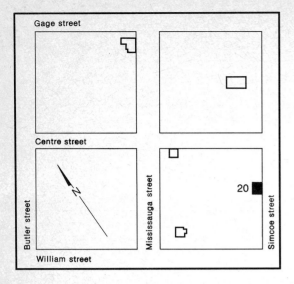

Gage street
Centre street
Butler street
Mississauga street
Simcoe street
William street
20

20

The Creen House

CIRCA 1817–25

363 Simcoe street

Owners of this property include the Breakenridge family, Garrett, and the Reverend Thomas Creen, who succeeded the Reverend Robert Addison to become the first rector of Niagara.

This is believed to be the oldest of the structures on the block: the nucleus of the present house was originally a gabled storey-and-a-half building, thirty-six feet by eighteen feet, with a large centre chimney. From this the house was extended to the south or left for twelve feet in the same form, then was increased in size for twelve feet across the back with a lean-to making the house into a saltbox except for a curious change in plans which produced an ell at the upper level at the south end. The alterations continued, stairs being relocated, openings changed, the chimneys eventually being erected in their present locations some time later. The composite tells an extremely complicated story of progressive adaptation from a small house, to school, and back to house. In recent preservation work even part of an old school desk with whittled edge, carved initials, and ink stains was found above the hall ceiling! For Mr Creen, a native of Ireland and educated at the University of Glasgow, was a Classics scholar and advertised for pupils, including boarders, in the 1820s. The changes did not stop there, but the puzzle was compounded continually as later owners made their contribution in coverings and minor modifications, needless to say often without catching up with the deficiencies inherent in the earlier construction.

The day of reckoning came, the investigations, the revelation of the building's history through progressive archaeology as it was dismantled. The decision was to rebuild much of it to the dimension and arrangement that formerly existed and in the process make such modifications as any owner would in improving his property, but in keeping with the original as an early nineteenth century carpenter might have done. So the essential character of the house has been preserved by careful attention to detail and with the knowledge of the original recorded and always at hand.

The exterior preserves its earlier form with tight eaves and verges giving it the appearance of early New England houses, particularly of those near the coast and also reminiscent of the simpler houses of the south. The house was originally painted a red ochre, then white after the chimneys were moved; its present deep ochre yellow is another traditional colour. The closed porch has given way to an open form, the old doorway to the dining room to a bay window. The rear bay window and lantern lighting the stairs are recent changes too. The coach house at the rear is a new building.

In the early house the plan had a centre hall; later the stair was placed within it, rising from the back of the house. To the left is now a drawing room, the former dining room, and to the right a sitting room, the former parlour, each with fireplace, and neat mantelpiece of pilaster and centre panel form. The alcoves are an added feature. To the left beyond the drawing room is the present dining room, possibly at one time serving as a schoolroom, and also with a fireplace. At the back, with its massive cooking fireplace signifying the old kitchen, is a family space now reserved as the keeping room, the small space beside it formerly a pantry and now the modern kitchen open to the larger room. Two other rooms are across the back, the larger still a bedroom. The stairs lead up to a large space from which the bedrooms open out; previously the upper rear room was connected to the bedrooms in the southern extension and probably by a back stair to the kitchen below.

St Andrew's is the least changed of the three principal churches of the town, and is always remembered when Niagara-on-the-Lake is recalled.

The building was to a design by Cooper, possibly a master builder serving as an architect, for the portico is a pure example of the Greek Doric style, and a very accomplished façade. It seems of English rather than American origin, the result of serious academic study and literal translation, unlike the innovative Greek of Asher Benjamin which is somewhat coarse. The front is grafted, oddly, to a purely Classical shell of brick with round-headed windows, while the tower is reminiscent of Wren's and Gibbs' London churches. In 1855 a windstorm severely damaged the roof, and the architect Kivas Tully recommended its reconstruction as a hipped form at the rear. In 1937 the Architectural Conservancy of Ontario, assisted financially by Thomas Foster, philanthropist and former mayor of Toronto, sponsored the restoration directed by Professor Eric R. Arthur.

The plan is rather unusual in that the pulpit is at the east end towards the street, and the congregation must enter on either side of it: no sneaking into the back pew unnoticed! The interior has box pews, little changed from the original layout. The gallery around three sides is supported on slender turned columns, the whole interior definitely Classical in feeling, but of the Renaissance and not the least bit Greek. The absence of a cornice at the ceiling seems strange but a mark exists about two feet down the wall which may indicate that this, or a broad cove, was removed, possibly after the roof was damaged in 1855.

The pulpitum was constructed in 1840 by the joiner, John Davidson, whose exquisite detailing in the native black walnut is still a masterpiece. Originally the minister emerged through the curtain at the back of the pulpit via a set of stairs from the vestry behind.

In the churchyard, as at St Mark's and St Vincent's, are many tombstones to evoke the interest of those concerned in the background of the town and its people, whose memory of memory and tale of tale have kept alive a history that is still in the making.

Nearby on the corner of Simcoe and Centre, is the manse constructed by Dr Robert McGill, the minister, in 1836. This is a neat hipped roof house of five bays, centre door with sidelight and fanlight, a storey and attic over a high basement in height.

21

St Andrew's Church

1831

Simcoe street

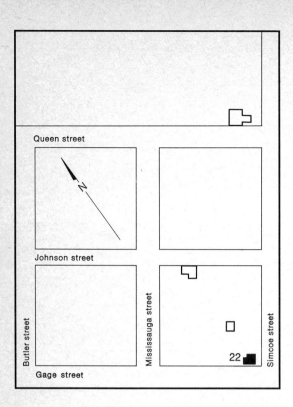

James Lockhart, the builder of this house, was a prominent merchant, banker, and ship-owner, and later the secretary of the Niagara Harbour and Dock Company. The house appears on the Vavasour map of 1817.

Here a brick house has been covered with stucco, finished smooth, and jointed to resemble cut stone: whether this was originally intended in the manner of the Regency, or was later applied to conceal a weatherbeaten and pockmarked east face, so common in the Ontario climate, is not known. Again, the two-storey gabled house with end chimneys and a five-bay front is typical of the Niagara scene, but the kitchen is in the rear wing forming the ell of the plan. Above the kitchen was a servants' loft.

The main section has the common centre hall layout with principal rooms to either side, now enlarged by including the smaller rooms which formerly existed behind these. The trim is simple, with mitred architraves, moulded with fine profiles as are chairrails and baseboards. The mantelpieces too are rather plain designs, with pilasters and centre panels, with fine reeding as the principal decoration on that in the dining room.

The present owner, in order to give greater storage space for books and china and his favourite objets d'art, had alcoves and bookcases fashioned by Carl Banke to complement the original detail of the interior.

22

Lockhart-Moogk House
CIRCA 1817 *Storrington*

289 Simcoe street

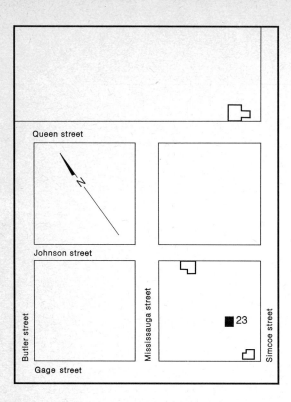

Queen street

Johnson street

Butler street

Mississauga street

Simcoe street

Gage street

■ 23

23

Butler House

CIRCA 1817

275 Simcoe street

The original owner could well have been Johnson Butler, magistrate, often referred to as 'Judge' Butler, whose name is such a nice blend of two great Loyalist family surnames from the Mohawk valley of upstate New York. The Butler House certainly befits such a personage. Its exterior is well proportioned, while not pretentious, its form of hip roof and large chimney stacks set inside the house simple yet substantial.

The building is a microcosm of the early Niagara house, with all the delightful details that this can contain, formal rooms well proportioned and neatly disposed, and a hall of generous dimensions. The form is almost a hip roofed 'cottage,' which became popular later in Canada West or Ontario, but here in a more distinguished example of the small house. It has a front of five bays with centre doorway, the basement set high to provide a kitchen below stairs as well as servants' quarters originally. The front was altered, probably about 1850, to give it a Greek Revival air, with pilastered trim to windows and panels below, a similarly trimmed doorway with heavy headboard and two panel door; the effect is recorded in a water-colour sketch by Owen Staples in 1911, and in Janet Carnochan's *History of Niagara* in 1913. Below this is the original clapboard finish, and elsewhere indicating the simpler early treatment. About 1850 the house was owned by a James Butler, farmer, whose family was fairly large: it was he who probably changed the front and must have added a wing – which obscured the rear windows and was later removed – to accommodate his children.

The interior is sheer delight, and reminds one of the beautiful parlour in the Farren House (51) at the end of King street. The front hall is decorated with an elaborate doorcase to the entrance, another at the back, a wooden cornice of intricate detail, chairrail, baseboard, and architraves all delicately moulded. To the left is the drawing room, its fireplace framed in a mantelpiece with colonettes, and

flanked by alcoves with fanlights above: trim here too is finely moulded, including the cornice at the ceiling. The front hall and drawing room are described by Janet Carnochan as decorated with 'grape leaves and grapes artistically painted.' Recent preservation work in the drawing room revealed a remarkable painted frieze with baskets of fruit centred at the top of each wall and cornucopias with peaches marching to the corners. A cartoon below the pier-glass rail between the windows provided a permanent urn of flowers above the table that would have been placed there. The theatre designer, Maurice Strike, has restored the painting to bring out its original colour; the vestiges in the hall were fragmentary and too badly perished to be saved.

On the right is the dining room, its fireplace originally with a crane, and with doors flanking the chimney breast. Here the windows are panelled below, the openings trimmed in an early form of symmetrically moulded pilaster with corner roundels, but the wooden cornice is a little simpler. Behind the hall a back hall leads to a bedroom on the left, heated originally by a stove, and another to the right with a fireplace, simpler mantel, and flanking cupboards. In the basement the cooking hearth and bakeoven have been reconstructed; the rest of the area has been given to additional living space and modern domestic comfort.

The Butler House stood formerly on part of the original Butler lands at the southern edge of town, at 590 Mississauga street, with little except great trees and shrubberies surrounding it. Removal to its present site has ensured its preservation for it was fast falling into dilapidation on its old site and no workable plan could be agreed upon to save it there. It retains most of its essential features and care has been taken to adapt it sympathetically.

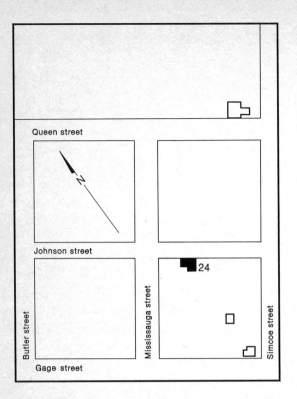

Perhaps the finest example of its type surviving in Niagara-on-the-Lake, the Clench House bespeaks the wealth and possession of a prominent Loyalist family. An earlier Clench House had miraculously been spared from the holocaust of 1813 sadly to be destroyed accidentally a few months later. Ralfe Clench began his new house, it is believed, some years after the War on Lot 114 which he had been granted as a Loyalist in 1796. The date of construction is not certain, and its elaborate trim suggests that it may have taken a long time to finish. Clench had been a lieutenant in Butler's Rangers, the first town clerk, was appointed a judge of the surrogate court in 1803 and was a member of the provincial parliament from 1806 to 1812. In the War he was a colonel in the Lincoln Militia and was taken prisoner. His wife, Elizabeth, was a granddaughter of Sir William Johnson. Ralfe Clench died in 1828.

The form of the building is a typical gable shape with interior chimneys having back-to-back fireplaces, the stacks serving perhaps to give added warmth to the house. The front, a very distinguished façade of five bays with a centre doorway ornamented with sidelights and fanlight and a Venetian window with sidelights above, faces the garden and One Mile Creek which meanders lazily across the two-acre plot. The front is elaborated with all the trimmings possible in a frame house, and seen elsewhere in buildings of comparable age like the Breakenridge-Hawley House (19) on Mississauga and the Crysler-Rigg House (15) on Queen. The fluted pilasters and Ionic caps support a simple cornice; the gable end is decorated with a pediment treatment with a loft light of a half ellipse, the original probably divided in a fan pattern. Although the front porch is a recent addition and extensions have been made in side balconies and a rear wing, the original still stands out in all its majesty.

The layout of the house with its centre hall favours the principal rooms to the front, with a kitchen originally in the high basement below, a sidehill position on the bank of the creek. Inside the house the glories continue, for few houses exhibit such a wealth of detail. Mantelpieces are exquisitely fashioned with colonettes and fanlike 'bat's wings' in the corners of the frieze, and carved and fluted elliptical fans adorn the fireplaces; the chimney breasts are flanked by alcoves with archways and decorated keystones, all exemplary of the finest joiner's craftsmanship. The spacious well-lit rooms, elegantly proportioned, the generous hall and its broad staircase, show the care and attention lavished upon a dwelling of the period.

24

Clench House

CIRCA 1824

234 Johnson street

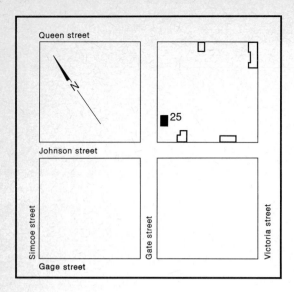

Three smaller houses and a cottage now form a fascinating group co-ordinated in the familiar black and white favoured in our time, but by no means indicative of the choice of colour in earlier times. If paint could be afforded at all white was expensive; its base, white lead, was frequently adulterated with less costly fillers and tinted with the earth pigments which give the familiar Venetian red, ochre yellow, or other mixtures still common on the Atlantic coast. However, Joseph Pickering in *Inquiries of an Emigrant (being the Narrative of an English Farmer)*, published in 1832, notes in his visit to the town in the summer of 1827: '... Monday, went to Niagara: the houses mostly frame, and painted white, with sash windows and Venetian blinds ...' (By Venetian blinds, it is thought, he meant louvred shutters.)

240 Gate street has undergone many changes and at one time was, like the Stewart-Anderson House (49), one of the few in Niagara with a chimney and fireplace in the south end. The present north chimney incorporates a fireplace saved intact from an old house dismantled for the fifth Welland Canal. The rest of the house has been treated with great sympathy by the last owner who employed a well-known local craftsman to contribute his handiwork to its preservation.

223 Gate street is probably a mid-nineteenth century example, and a simple house of salt-box shape. The cottage by One Mile Creek, 243 Gate, is believed to be the latest in the group. Its diminutive size and ordered simplicity lend it the endearing charm of a doll's house.

25

MacMonigle-Craik House

CIRCA 1818

240 Gate street

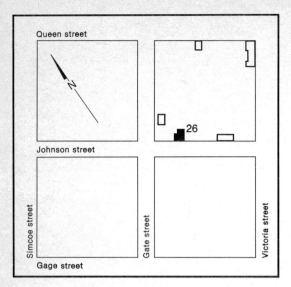

5

In connection with many early buildings, the transactions involving subdivision of acre lots to provide new house sites became very complicated and subsequent dealings often confuse the original plots. The west half-acre of Lot 99 on which both the MacMonigle-Craik House (25) and this house stand belonged to Joseph Adnams, joiner, from 1811 until this quarter was sold in 1816 to John Mac-Monigle (MacMannigle or MacMonigal), variously described as gardener and yeoman. In turn, in 1821 MacMonigle sold a small lot, on which this house was built facing Johnson street, to George Greenlees. The plot was then enlarged in 1829 by the addition of the corner property formerly occupied by MacMonigle (then spelt MacMonigal), and sold in 1833 at greatly increased value, to Lewis Donally, indicating improvements by that time.

The Greenlees-Craik House is another early building in the familiar position tight to the street. The exterior detail is plain, the façade a simple balanced arrangement of entrance door near the centre and window on each side, the arrangement of openings repeated in the windows above: the slight asymmetry provides greater width for the room on the right. Its gable form of two storeys with large end chimneys indicates the four fireplaces the house still retains. Eaves appear to have been changed, and possibly the doorcase has lost its transom.

Although the interior is for the most part very simple, three finely decorated mantelpieces of excellent craftsmanship do survive. However, it is remarkable that such massive chimney breasts were suffered to remain in so small a house.

26

Greenlees-Craik House

CIRCA 1822

135 Johnson street

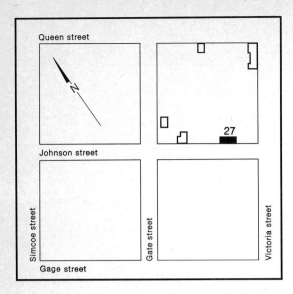

6

The only terrace or row houses left in Niagara are these on Johnson although others are reported, one survives on Picton but two houses have been made from the original three, and another group was subsequently moved back and redivided on the next block on Johnson. The position follows the town tradition – right on the street.

In 1832 the land was sold to George Varey, a tailor, for many years the player of the bass viol at the services in the Methodist church. Possibly it was he who built these houses some years later as an investment while living in the finer house on the north-west corner of Johnson and Victoria streets. The plot of three-quarters of an acre remained in the Varey family almost until the end of the century.

Interiors are similar in all three, with a small hall, parlour to the front, a keeping room with cooking fireplace behind, a tight stair to two or three small rooms upstairs. Behind is a small lean-to or wing. These are strictly workers' houses, probably built originally for rent and minimum accommodation for a small family. The present owner, to provide more space for his family, has joined two of the houses together without altering the façade.

There is no pretension, and the bare essential of detail, but the common vernacular expression produces a building of unity, a neat front to the street. The finish in the old red ochre is a traditional colour of early frame buildings. Examination of the framing some years ago revealed large beams and posts, possibly from some other building or intended for a larger structure, for they seemed of inordinate size.

27

Varey-Thalmann Houses

CIRCA 1840

115-19 Johnson street

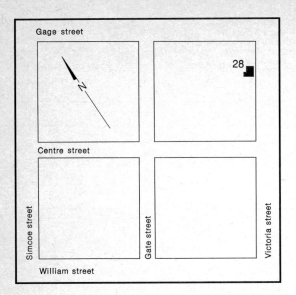

George A. Clement, yeoman, sold the part of Lot 153, now known as 315 Victoria street, to Henry Carlisle, a tailor, in 1848 for a sum indicating land without a building.

This one-and-a-half storey frame house with its three-bay front and centre door is an example of the medium sized dwelling of the mid-nineteenth century, built for an owner probably of moderate means and no great pretensions. Yet it is good looking, well proportioned, and speaks much for the tradition still entrenched in the local vernacular of the time.

The interior is relatively simple, following the usual centre hall arrangement, a parlour to the right of the front door and a bedroom behind, the dining room to the left and kitchen at the back. The staircase balustrade, substantial in design, is supported at the base by a 'seahorse' newel, a block of wood carved into a sinuous S curve. No fireplaces are evident: by the time this house was built the reliance upon stoves was complete.

The neat porch to this house came from the Vanderlip-Marcy House (30) almost two blocks away, and was probably moved when new sidewalks were constructed about 1910.

28

Carlisle-Brook House

CIRCA 1850

315 Victoria street

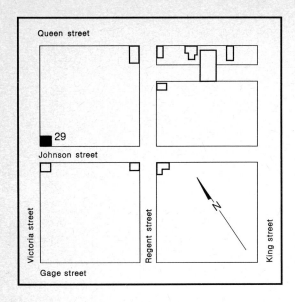

Fortunately some buildings are documented, but few are as conveniently chronicled as this one with the date carved in the keystone over the front door. With incontrovertible evidence like this it is no wonder that this house serves as a touchstone for Niagara's architectural history. This substantial yet simple brick residence has a certain quality of permanence and commodity about it. The large windows give the interior a feeling of airiness, albeit the rooms, though well proportioned, are not very large. Only the front entrance has any attention given to it, a well detailed six-panel door, with a semi-circular fanlight above, the arched surround supported by fluted pilasters. The house has chimney stacks at each end; the roof is a hipped form of low pitch.

Even casual examination of the exterior will identify a corner opening to the building believed to have served as an office entrance when Mr Connell was the postmaster. The house was built by a master mason, James Blain, who, like the carpenter, John Davidson, was engaged in many building projects in the town.

The interior is the familiar centre hall, with principal rooms complete with fireplaces to the front, lesser rooms behind. Originally the main stair was supplemented by a smaller side stair connecting the basement kitchens with the ground and second floors allowing the servants access out of view. The kitchens are curious with two sets of cooking arrangements, each with fireplace and bakeoven adjacent, which seems a concession to the odd marvellous party. However, in spite of the chimney arrangement, there is still the common layout on the west side of the house facing Victoria street with the fireplaces on the centre wall in basement and ground floor, while upstairs a corner fireplace occurs on the stack as it twists to emerge at the end of the house.

The interior detail shows a preference for symmetrical pilastered trims and corner

blocks with foliate ornament in the main rooms, and again simpler mitred trim to inferior spaces. However the ceiling cornices are linear designs also with foliate decoration in corner paterae, a detail helping to corroborate the date of the Lyons-Jones House (58) at Centre and King where a similar treatment is seen.

The Post House and its neighbour the Varey-Middleditch House across Victoria street seem to frame the corner so admirably, a feature to be repeated but a block away by houses of similar shape and general design (31 & 32). Originally the Varey-Middleditch House, c1837 was a centre hall plan too, the front doorcase a detail with sidelights and rectangular transom above. The principal rooms are on either side of the hall, the drawing room to the right with a fireplace, the dining room to the left obviously with a stove while the kitchen behind had a cooking hearth. Mr Varey was a tailor and his workroom, with shelf-marks on the wall, appears to have been in the north-east corner of the house, a window to north and east, the walls painted a deep red ochre, a colour reproduced in the south-west room. The building has been restored to a single-family dwelling from an earlier 20th-century conversion to a double house. Its roughcast finish was common to Regency houses, and has been reproduced. The hipped roof and simple outline give a neat and trim appearance. A building appears on the site in Gray's 1810 map: examination of the foundation showed the stone to be spalled on the face as would occur in the intense heat of a fire, so this part of the house may be a relic of pre-War days.

29

Blain-Lansing House
1835 *The Post House*

95 Johnson street

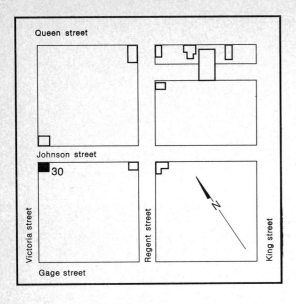

An old photograph shows this house to be in a sad state, without paint and much in need of care. Care has in fact now been lavished on it and the house hardly resembles that former aspect, thanks to a previous owner, and the hand of a local craftsman. As in many other early buildings undergoing preservation to keep them in active use, some changes have occurred: for example, the insertion of upper storey windows along the front for better light and ventilation to bedrooms. The interior is a particularly charming example of how older buildings may be adapted to modern convenience.

The house is the familiar centre hall with a simple staircase in a straight flight. The principal rooms, with their original detail, survive on either side, somewhat enlarged by taking in ground floor sleeping space. The hearth to the left may have served a keeping room where most daily activity took place, for the owner discovered what appeared to be a bake-oven on the back of this chimney, indicating perhaps a former kitchen lean-to. This arrangement resembles the ground floor plan of the Moore-Bishop-Stokes House (48).

Again this building stands right on the street: its old porch on the line of the newer sidewalk was removed to the Carlisle-Brook House (28) on Victoria street. Legend has it that this house was the only one to have escaped the burning of 1813, but recent research places a doubt here: another old frame house on a plot on the other side of Victoria is believed to have survived to be torn down ignominiously early in this century!

30

Vanderlip-Marcy House

CIRCA 1816

96 Johnson street

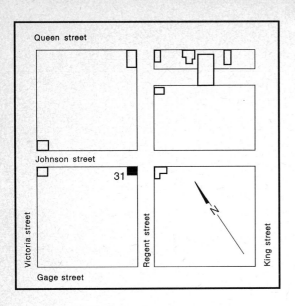

Like the Blain-Lansing House (29) and its neighbour this is one of a pair of houses forming an impressive 'gateway' to a cross street. The three-bay front of this building with its two-storey hipped roof form and interior chimneys is a familiar local pattern. Restoration of essential features has begun and the illustration indicates the final appearance. The doorway, with its generous treatment of panelled reveals, sidelights, and expansive fanlight, spells a welcome. The design of the doorcase is somewhat similar to that on the Richardson-Kiely House (16).

The centre hall plan is, again, typical with one particular difference here in the position of the fireplace across the inside corner of the room, practically speaking the optimum for heating and aesthetically a fascinating change. Interior trim is of the two types: the symmetrical pilastered form with corner blocks, and simpler mitred designs. The mantelpieces are elegant though simple, and rather high. The stair is a broad, straight flight with a simple balustrade, the coarse turned newel at the bottom, however, suggesting either an inexpert hand or a later change; when the hall was painted in Prussian blue this was almost lost to view. Nevertheless, upstairs elegant tapered newels of an earlier period survive and this, with the curious medley of trim, seems to indicate re-use of older material or a certain laxity in previous refurbishing.

31

Jones-Eckersley-Brownell House

CIRCA 1833

58 Johnson street

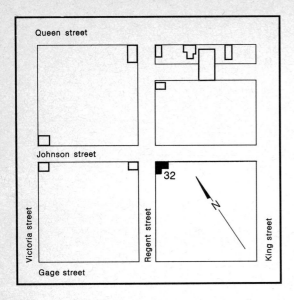

The other 'post' to the 'gateway,' and balancing the Jones-Eckersley-Brownell House (31), is a building of similar form, and originally comparable clapboard finish. Now apartments, but with much of its rather rich detail still intact, this house is a worthy example of the town. The door knocker, of polished brass, has the name 'Barker Hall' engraved on it, after John Barker, a prominent municipal official who built the house.

Instead of the rigid symmetry usually seen in such a frontal treatment some leeway has been practised to allow a larger room to the right of the doorway, putting the hall slightly off-centre dimensionally. The exterior is basically simple in detail with attention concentrated upon the fine doorcase with its slender attenuated columns or colonettes, fluted, and supporting a narrow cornice forming the transom. The sash above is decorated in a lozenge pattern, a less common design locally. The panelled treatment of the chimney stacks is a noteworthy local feature.

Inside, the staircase represents the local joiner's work with its well executed scroll and balustrade and good proportions. The trim, elaborate, some delicately undercut, and principally of the pilastered type decorated with foliate corner blocks, follows the typical fashion of the decade 1825 to 1835 and fits well with the moulded six-panel doors. The mantelpieces with bold colonettes and elliptical fan paterae are part of the mode, and the simpler designs with pilasters and centre panels are relegated to lesser rooms.

32

Barker Hall

CIRCA 1831

46 Johnson street

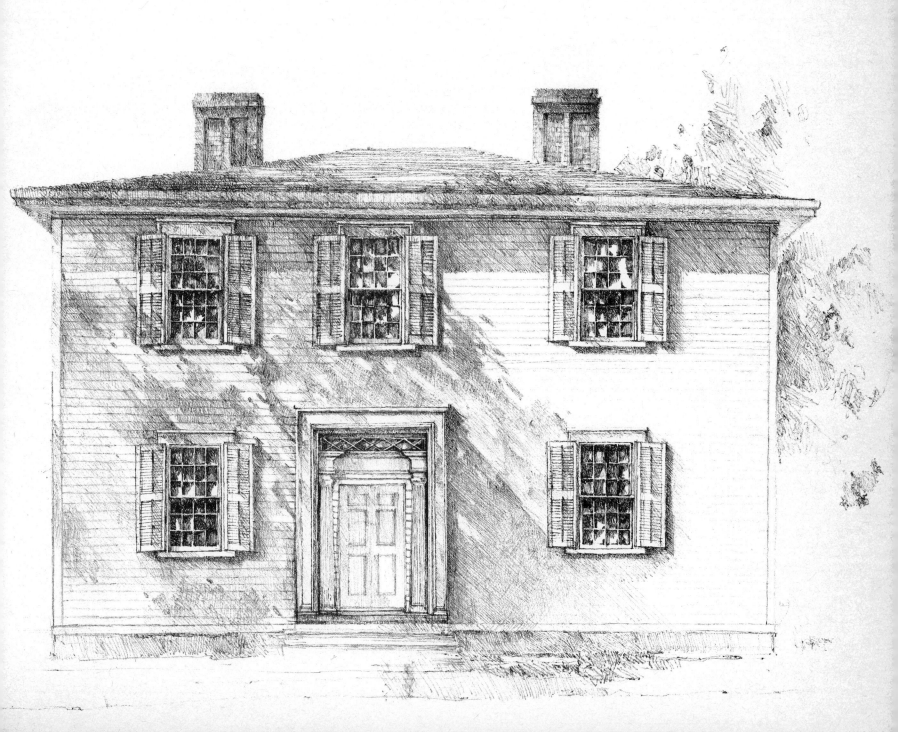

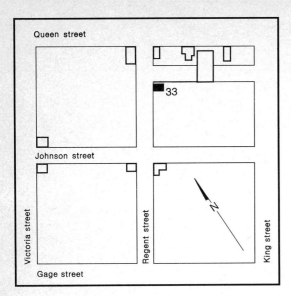

Yet another tavern lends force to Mrs Jameson's concern for the character of the town. The Angel Inn was erected on part of the old Town plot inherited from the Crown which had purchased D.W. Smith's residence for Government House, a building facing King street and burnt in 1813. The property was deeded to the Town for its purposes and the street frontages were originally leased by the magistrates, and only recently sold off to private owners: the resulting complexity is extremely difficult to understand. In Janet Carnochan's *History of Niagara*, R. Howard is stated to have been the proprietor from 1826 to 1846 when he moved to keep the Promenade House (4) at Prideaux and Regent. Then, the same author remarks, the tavern was kept by John Fraser who changed the name to the Mansion House. Also in this history it is noted to have been a meeting place of the Freemasons at one time.

The Angel Inn is a timber-framed building covered in more recent years with pebbledash but originally, as an old photograph of *c*1900 shows, with clapboard finish. The building is a full two storeys, with gables, and a rather unusual asymmetrical front of four bays resulting in an off-centre doorway. An interior chimney rising behind the roof ridge probably served back-to-back fireplaces in the rooms to the left of the front door. A doorway at the end may well have led to the tap room. Perhaps the kitchen was to the rear.

Trim, although simple for the most part, did include a mantelpiece, now on display in the Museum, and was of typical local design: the stair is a straight flight with little elaboration.

33

The Angel Inn
CIRCA 1825

Market street

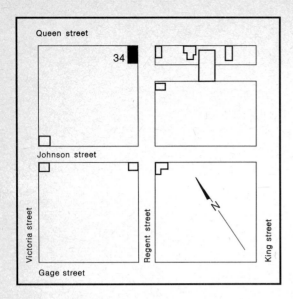

In 1843 William H. Dee, a merchant obtained a substantial mortgage from Elizabeth Dee, widow, signifying the construction of some improvement to lot 67, on which this building stands. In 1865 Elizabeth Dee sold the corner piece of the property occupied by John Mc-Culloch to Henry Paffard, the man who in 1866 moved his chemist's shop to the renovated premises now restored as the Niagara Apothecary (1) at Queen and King streets.

The neat, much-divided, storefront on the Regent street façade of this building is indicative of the design of pre-1850 commercial enterprises of the town. It once housed a bakeshop. The Queen street front with its cut-stone pilasters and carved caps is a handsome treatment for any store range and shows the early nineteenth century concern for order and the appropriate expression. With the upper windows restored, its simple dignity is evident. At one time James Lockhart is said to have operated a branch of the Commercial Bank in these premises.

Above and along the side the brickwork is carefully laid in the decorative pattern of Flemish bond as befitted the street fronts of buildings of the time. The neat arrangement of the original second floor windows contrasts with later extensions and embellishments.

However, the interior has lost its original detail to be replaced by late nineteenth century trim in rather drastic alterations. A vestige of a moulding typical of the period 1835 to 1850 exists behind the old storefront to the side of the building.

34

Dee-LeDoux Building

CIRCA 1843

54-8 Queen street

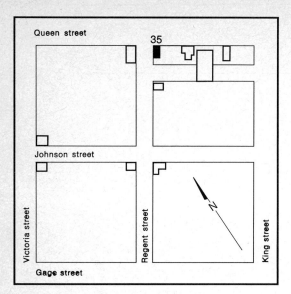

Queen street

35

Johnson street

Victoria street

Regent street

King street

Gage street

The buildings along Queen street flanking the Court House were erected by merchants also on land leased from the town, and only recently were these sold as freeholds.

In 1825 John J. Daly advertized in the *Gleaner* that he had removed his premises to the new brick store opposite Mr John Young's: it is believed this refers to the brick building on the south-east corner of Queen and Regent, possibly one of the earliest in the block. Daly, like his successor Alma, was a general merchant.

Alma's Store, still with its arcaded front of two storeys, long and rather narrow divided windows, and gable ends with parapets and chimneys appears in a pre-1875 photographic view. A front gable with crane beam indicates the use of the upper storeys for storage. Rows of barrels along Regent street point to the store of a wine and spirit merchant, the prominent T sign on the side designating him as a general provisioner. Looking carefully you can still discern the arcading in the upper storeys filled in to match its neighbour constructed in the mid or late 1870s.

The Alma family later inhabited the Stewart House (3), at Prideaux and Regent only a block away.

In the same block, immediately to the east of the Court House, is another brick building with arcaded treatment along the side, said to have been the location of W.D. Miller, stationer, who lived in the Miller House (50) at Mary and Regent. In 1828 Robert Dickson, barrister, advertizes that he has taken those premises formerly occupied by Mr Miller. However, the detail of sills and window heads above is similar to that seen on buildings erected in St Catharines in the late 1840s and early 1850s, perhaps indicating a second storey addition or rebuilding about this time.

35

Alma's Store

1825 *The Yardstick*

46 Queen street

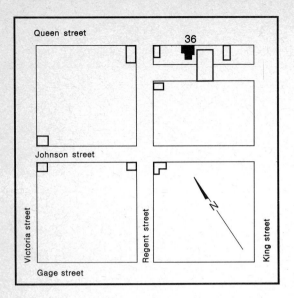

Queen street

36

Johnson street

Victoria street

Regent street

King street

Gage street

Next to the Court House is a later 'boomtown' front whose form is curious until a little analysis and conjecture tries to make sense of the amalgam. The surviving mid-Victorian shopfront, although a charming and sympathetic detail to our eyes, is probably not the original but a change during the renovation which unified two separate buildings. The originals were possibly similar with gable ends to the street, a shopfront with three windows above. The space between the two buildings appears then to have been filled in to provide access to the upper floor, the side roofs extended to provide an attic over the centre. Then, as if in embarrassment or chagrin at this minor insult to the street, or an attempt to reduce the ungainliness of the composite, the façade appears to have been redressed in a mock front with horizontal cornice treatment.

Between the Sherlock Block and Alma's Store is a neat row of typical main street fronts of the mid nineteenth century; unfortunately the ground floor has been modernized, somewhat unsympathetically, but the upper storey is still in clapboard. The old photograph revealing Alma's Store and the Sign of the Pineapple (38) shows this building with a typical house in its western half (to the right) with centre door and window on each side, while the eastern half was a divided shopfront appropriate to the period.

36

Sherlock Block

CIRCA 1850

34-6 Queen street

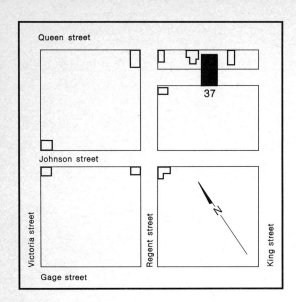

Queen street
Johnson street
Gage street
Victoria street
Regent street
King street
37

37

The Court House

1847

Queen street

The Court House, whose architect was William Thomas, was one of the last acts of the County of Lincoln toward the original seat of government! Niagara lost out to its rapidly growing rival, St Catharines, on the new, and second, Welland Canal. So Niagara's Court House became its Town Hall, and St Catharines' Town Hall, by Thomas' rival, the architect Kivas Tully, was enlarged to become the Lincoln County Court House!

Thomas' presentation drawings are preserved on detail paper, all carefully drawn at small scale to indicate the layout, and coloured to make them more legible. Elevations appear to have been lost or destroyed; rather a pity for intent can no longer be compared to actuality. The building plan has been adapted in the course of years to serve more as a centre for community activities, which lately have included not only the temporary quarters of the Shaw Festival during the summer season, but for annual events such as the Simcoe Ball staged by the Niagara Historical Society and more recently the Kettle Drum, a traditional gathering of local bons vivants sponsored by the same group. Dances, meetings, and suppers are constant happenings in the Court House.

Thomas' drawing shows the elaboration of the Court Room arrangements on the second floor and indicates a central domed ceiling. With the interesting barrel vault in the lesser hall behind, this is quite conceivable. The plan included a market hall at the back on the ground floor: this was later a fire hall and is now the Public Library. The cell and staircase arrangements have been modified, and other losses have occurred such as the cupola that decorated the top of the Court Room roof. Mr Thomas thoughtfully provided for water closets in his new building: the location survives, somewhat newly plumbed.

Externally the building is a fine example of the Classical Revival considered suitable to a civic building: had it been a church or a collegiate structure both Mr Thomas and Mr Tully might have favoured Gothic. There is a certain aspect of the eclectic which permeates the whole, with detail and ornament like the bracketted cornice borrowed rather freely; though effectively combined, the purity and freshness of earlier domestic building in the local vernacular is lacking. Nevertheless the bold treatment of stonework is well handled and the arrangement of openings pleasantly devised. Unfortunately the massing is hard to recognize because of impinging building along the street and this may account for its somewhat split identity in the frontal façade and the rear wing joined by a rather inconsequential link.

Some interior detail does survive to indicate the grandeur of its original finish, and the imposing doorways in the ground floor passage and columns to the back contrast with the simple, austere mantel designs in marble. Only vestiges of detail remain in the Court Room although the staircase to it appears to be a survival of the original.

The clock tower erected as a war memorial in front of the present Town Hall, like many a cause before and after, almost tore the citizenry asunder; it was the subject of much bitter debate, not only for its expense and its supposed impropriety but also for its design. Admitted that the Niagara area has a curious penchant for diminutive campanile, this device serves an admirable purpose in the local townscape: it forms a focal point for Queen, the ninety-nine foot main street, formerly almost without end. True, it might have been an Egyptian obelisk had it been built in an earlier period and a European situation, or a classical column of academic purity; whatever we think let us be thankful it was not a granite howitzer or stone lad in puttees.

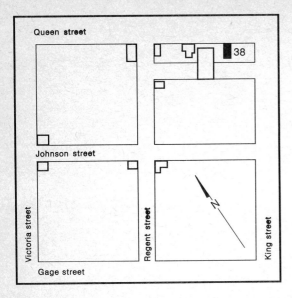

Queen street in Niagara-on-the-Lake illustrates what has sometimes been termed the 'primitive' or 'informal' commercial street as opposed to the 'formal' treatment of matching or similar façades represented by a town such as Port Hope, Ontario, where private and speculative development over the period 1840 to 1870 produced a rare and rather magnificent street spectacle of regular fronts in brick. 'Primitive' is intended to convey the reverse of 'formal,' of individual versus common concern in appearances: it is, as it were, every man for himself. The consequences are obvious, the street architecturally is more picturesque and organic than disciplined. Only the common elements of window proportions and position, cornices, and detail tend to hold the effect together and when these are destroyed the result is dull and disorderly, to become even banal when new – and unsympathetic – materials are callously applied in misguided attempts to modernize.

So the Sign of the Pineapple shoots above its neighbours in three storeys of heavy timber framing. The original shopfront was probably a myriad of small window panes, but the preservation has sought to be sympathetic, by invoking the scale and detail of the Gothic Revival to represent a late Regency or early Victorian renewal.

An old photograph, taken before 1875, which shows Alma's Store (35) at Queen and Regent with its original windows and arcaded front, also indicates this building in the background. At that time the top floor must have been simply a storage loft for the year's supplies, for a centre door with crane beam and hook protruding from a gable in the roof above is clearly evident. On the inside, the mark of the centre opening could still be seen prior to recent renovations. One interesting detail is the tinted glass in the front windows, an amethyst grey cast rather like that in Boston's Beacon Hill, but here probably a glass of less than prime quality.

38

The Sign of the Pineapple

CIRCA 1830

16 Queen street

History records that this building served from fairly early days as the Bank of Upper Canada: the remains of a later vault are still in the basement. The previous building on the site had been known as the Yellow House, presumably referring to its colour which was probably the soft ochre sometimes used on early buildings, and had served for some time prior to the War as an inn. From 1854 to 1873 the property was owned by Lewis Shickluna, the shipbuilder.

Although the exterior is a somewhat chastened and altered form of the original, the indication of original sash helps to bring the building back into focus. Probably clapboard for the early finish, the smooth ashlar-lined stucco of the front and roughcast of the sides at present reflect a mid or later nineteenth century preference and an attempt to reduce maintenance.

Some of the interior survives, but much has been changed. The early centre hall plan still governs the layout, but extensions and reworking have contributed many minor changes. The present verandah is a decidedly late nineteenth century 'embellishment.' The building is now a guest house.

39

Bank of Upper Canada

CIRCA 1817

10 Front street

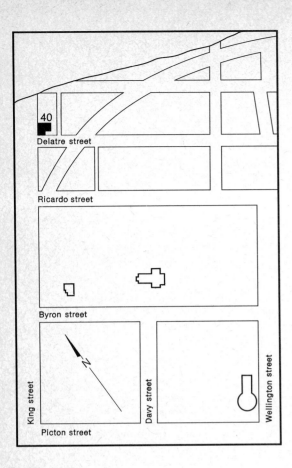

40

The Whale Inn

1835

66 King street

The Whale Inn, as it was known originally (more recently it has been referred to as the Elliott House), figures in some early sketches of the foot of King street. Apparently it was built as an hotel to cater to the sailors and travellers who frequented the port and town.

Of two storeys, with a five-bay front, gable roof, and slight chimneys at the end and a rear wing of a storey and a half housing the old kitchen, the Whale Inn remains largely intact from the exterior. The tap room door on the left of the front suggests a tavern. The centre doorway is an example of the simple type with pilasters, sidelights, and deep frieze below a cornice. The oval device with clasped hands over the door is a fire insurance mark identifying the insured at a time when private fire fighting companies would protect only their own customers. Windows are with the larger panes more easily and cheaply obtainable by this time. Eaves returns and the distinct indication of a built-in gutter along the cornices at the edge of the roof highlight another common local detail only too often lost by neglect. The gable end openings of quarter circles lighting the loft are another common decorative feature, and more often these were divided in the form of a fan.

The building has a centre hall with stair, the tap room to the left, parlour to the right and a large kitchen down half a flight to the wing at the back. Here is the only fireplace in the building, a cooking hearth, the rest of the space being heated by stoves and the accompanying web of stovepipes. The trim is simple with moulding of a profile first seen in the early 1830s and to remain popular in slightly different form for over fifty years.

Early in the 1950s the house was in a sad state, although it had served for over a century as one of the well-known hostelries of Niagara. Then a new owner, ably assisted by a well known local craftsman, restored much of its original quality; since then it has been a very comfortable and pleasant house.

Archdeacon MacMurray, the third to serve St Mark's, and the second rector of Niagara seems to have been the instigator of the Rectory, for the building was constructed a year after he reached the parish. Previously Mac-Murray had been at Dundas and as a young man had ministered to the Indians at Sault Ste Marie where his first wife, part Indian herself, was a great help to him. His name appears in the annals of the Old Stone House built by Charles Oakes Ermatinger at the Sault. Previously the rector had his own private house: for example, the Reverend Thomas Creen, who lived on Simcoe street (20), and the Reverend Robert Addison whose farmhouse dating from before the War, a haven and centre of church life during the conflict, still stands on the shore of the lake to the west of the town.

The Anglican Rectory, the town's only Tuscan villa, is an example of a very popular house design of the mid-nineteenth century. Constructed in pressed buff brick, an early use of this material, the building always looks clean and fresh. The square tower and wide bracketted eaves are of the period and follow a pattern first seen in some of John Nash's early Regency villas and small country houses and much favoured by American designers like Andrew Jackson Downing and his followers.

Note the builder's, or the architect's, difficulty in arranging the tower windows where the vertical alignment over the second storey places the openings off-centre above. The panelled chimneys are the original, bold massive designs adding interest to the silhouette. The porch appears to be later, and a verandah was probably a detail of the original. The chimney positions reflect the rather conventional local plan that forms the basis of the layout, with the fireplaces on the inside walls. Originally with a basement kitchen, the present arrangement uses what was probably a small dining room or morning room for that purpose, while the principal rooms, the drawing room and dining room, face the garden at the back of the house. The hall is central to the layout with the rooms arranged in an ell plan around it.

The detail in the building is somewhat simpler than earlier houses of the town, the mouldings broad and the trim heavy, characteristic of the mid-century. The rooms are high ceilinged, with French windows to the rear verandah from the main rooms. Plaster cornices are bold, mantelpieces plain with pilasters and simple trim of the room. Tower rooms are usually a delight of such houses and here this is true – a marvellous place to grow up in. The finest detail of the house is the magnificent spiral staircase which makes a steep sweep out of the hall, its graceful curve echoed by the plaster of the underside and the flight of the balustrade with full handrail and turned vase shape balusters of oak.

41

The Rectory

1858

17 Byron street

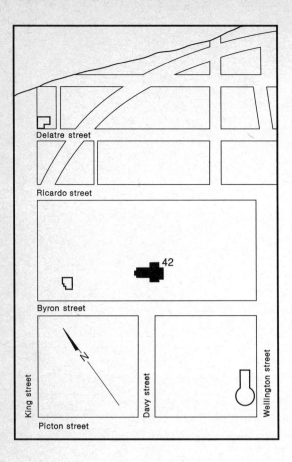

The Church of St Mark tells the story of a building in transition, the history of its changes still clearly visible within the fabric itself. In recent preservation work nothing was done to conceal the telltale marks of alterations: their presence was mute reminder of the evolution to this day.

In plan St Mark's is now cruciform, a traditional shape. Originally, however, it was rectangular with an apsidal east end, a form shown in an early sketch and still traceable in the floor at the nave side of the crossing. This section constructed between 1804 and 1810 was used as a barracks and hospital during the War and gutted in the fire of 1813. The stone walls survived and the church was rebuilt, to be finished after a great struggle in 1822. In 1828 the church was at last consecrated. By the 1840s Niagara's population was steadily rising, the Church of England congregation too, and plans were put in hand to enlarge St Mark's with transepts and chancel in 1843, with galleries inserted and the two high pulpits that survive. At this time the theme of the original classic exterior was followed and, although the barrel vaulted ceiling was retained, the interior showed the influence of the Gothic in the treatment of pulpits and the tracery of the new east window whose stained glass is probably about this time. Box pews, however, still served the congregation.

The next major change occurred in 1892 when, after anything but unanimous support, the galleries were swept away, the choir and organ jammed into the chancel, and the box pews replaced by the present benches, their remains to become the panelled wainscoat surround. Stained glass windows gradually replaced the many panes of clear glass similar to those still to be seen in the vestry.

In 1964 a crack in the ceiling signified that the roof had been held up by an act of Providence for some years and that drastic repairs were necessary. The rebuilding of the ceiling, lighting, relocation of organ and choir in the gallery, the new altar arrangements, the font with cover by Jacobine Jones, the magnificent window by Yvonne Williams, and the redecoration of the church date from this time, when Mr Harry Mansfield was rector.

A walk around the churchyard reveals many fascinating old tombstones with the names of the early settlers of Niagara among them, for this was originally the town burial ground too. The peace and quiet of this spot with its magnificent trees is a welcome respite from the noisy bustle of the modern metropolis.

42

St Mark's Church

1805 & 1843

Byron street

9

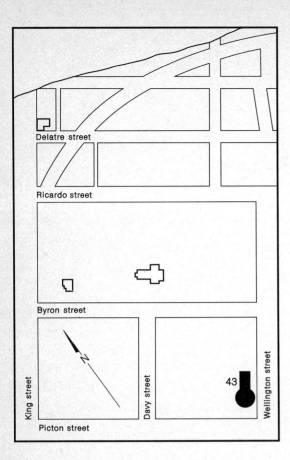

The three denominations, Presbyterian, Church of England, and Roman Catholic, were each granted large blocks of land in the town for their churches and churchyards. The Roman Catholics had theirs next to the square which became the town space, Simcoe Park.

Here in 1834 they began a church, of timber, sheathed in clapboard, with a tower crowned by a steeple at its 'western' end. The church had pointed windows, and in all respects subscribed to the popular notion of what was proper for ecclesiastical work – a preference for the Gothic Revival.

The interior is a particular delight, especially when viewed in the soft light of late afternoon or early evening when the warm, diffused colour radiates a warmth of communion that few can forget. The older part of the church has been largely preserved on the inside, a stipulation of the donor, the late Mr R.O. Petman, who provided for the enlargement of the church in 1965 as a memorial to his first wife.

The groined vaulting all in wood is particularly interesting. The curious compromise of its supporting pilasters ornamented in the pointed shapes of the Gothic Revival topped by a species of Ionic cap – obviously its creator was still classically inclined – is surely fascinating, the best way to enjoy both worlds, in this and the next!

The additions to the church in 1965 were necessitated by the growing parish and it was then that the changes to furniture were made. The gallery, in its original position from the old church, serves as the bridge between the two parts; the new extension of the nave was determined by the need to preserve as much as possible of the older building. Only the tower was lost, and the former 'west' wall is marked by the strip of blue marble in the floor.

43

Church of St Vincent de Paul

1834

Picton street

I

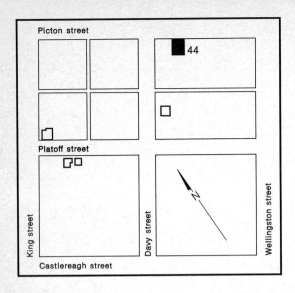

The area east of King street is referred to as the New Survey, being granted by the Crown to James Crooks in exchange for his lands confiscated in the Military Reserve to build Fort Mississauga. The property was divided and sold by the Crooks family to various owners after the War, mostly after 1825.

Richard Moffat purchased his lot at the corner of Picton and Davy in 1834 and took a mortgage about the same time – probably indicating his intention to build. In 1855 the building was still described as Moffat's Hotel.

In the mid 1830s Niagara was still a prosperous place with people engaged in building fine houses or renovating the interiors of those built just after the War, a place of bustling commerce, a new industry, the shipyard, growing, and with little fear of that experimental ditch, the first Welland Canal.

Moffat's Hotel is indicative of the simple, ordered vernacular of Upper Canada of the time, with its centre doorway flanked by two windows and a range of five above. An extension to the rear for the full width of the front provided additional space. The main kitchen was apparently in the basement with cooking hearth and bakeoven; the heavy chimney stack attests to this and the large fireplaces once in the building. Clapboard is probably the original finish, stucco possible as a later covering. The doorway, represented elsewhere in the town, would have had a panelled door with sidelights separated by pilasters and deep headboard or frieze above: traces of the design are clearly evident. Sashes for the most part have survived.

44

Moffat's Hotel

CIRCA 1835

60 Picton street

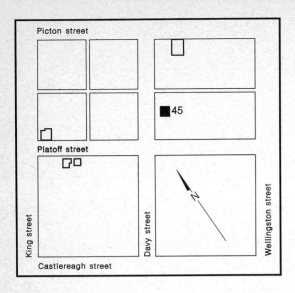

Part of James Crooks' New Survey, this property, originally a quarter of an acre, was purchased by Peter Baikie, shipwright, in 1842, a year after he sold his holding on Platoff to Malcolmson (47).

The Baikie House indicates a new departure, the almost universal preference at the time for a verandah: the long French windows appear to have been planned for it. The fretwork ornament may be slightly later, but its intricacy suggests a shipwright's whimsy. The upper sash indicate a later Victorian change.

The shallow shape of the house follows another Niagara precedent with the single room on either side of the hall and the kitchen behind in a lean-to. By this period the fireplace had been abandoned for the more efficient and more economical stove as a source of heat.

45

Baikie-Borsook House

CIRCA 1842

230 Davy street

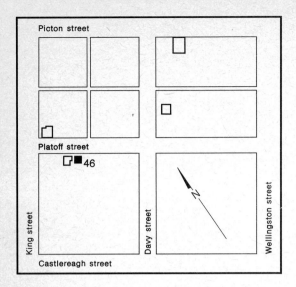

In 1835 James Crooks sold the lot on which this house stands to Henry Sewell, a carpenter, whose son Thomas, the publisher, subdivided the property, selling this portion to Thomas Dover late in 1838. The property was bought by Edward Dixon, carpenter, in 1842, with the increase in value registered in the transaction suggesting that a small house existed on the property at that time. It changed hands again in 1844, being purchased by Thomas Eedson, also a carpenter. Until this time it had been a tiny lot of thirty feet along the street by fifty feet in depth, a very small space when municipal services of water supply and the like were not known. However, Eedson had purchased the adjoining property on King street, part of which was retained and added to this plot.

More recently this board and batten cottage, very much weatherbeaten, was pronounced virtually impossible to preserve: it took a former owner many months to bring it back to 'life,' and it has never ceased to be coveted since.

This is a very simple small house, the front door opening into a larger room, with two small bedrooms originally off this. In the lean-to part of the saltbox behind was the kitchen with a stair to a loft in the roof of the main section. A little fine detail survived, including a small mantelpiece, but the conversion has added new and enjoyable dimensions for a small household. The external board and batten finish is typical of the mid nineteenth century and may have replaced earlier clapboard.

46

Dover-Daly House

CIRCA 1839

20 Platoff street

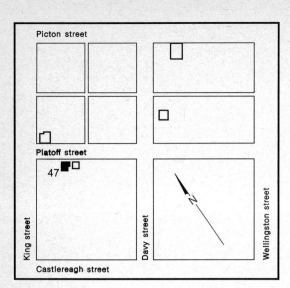

This, like the neighbouring Dover property, started out as a subdivision of the Sewell lot in the New Survey purchased from James Crooks, this part of the property passing to Peter Baikie, a shipwright, in 1838. In 1841 Baikie sold to James Malcolmson for a slightly increased sum, perhaps signifying the start of a house; the property had again accrued in value by 1853 when it changed hands once again to Walter J. McNeilly.

The house is another small dwelling typical of the town. The exterior is simple, with no pretension at all, but the relationship of windows, though by no means perfect from the standpoint of studied composition, is not unpleasant and the façade has a discipline about it that is restful to the eye and mannerly to its neighbours. The interior, too, is extremely simple, and the layout typical.

47

Malcolmson-Walker House

CIRCA 1845

16 Platoff street

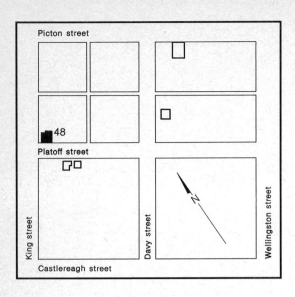

This building is located also in the 'new' part of the town, east of King street, granted to James Crooks. In 1828 the lot on which the house stands was purchased by Francis Moore, yeoman, who then involved himself in a mortgage suggesting a building operation. In 1848 it passed on to Mr Thomas Doritty or Dority, recorded as a tavernkeeper at the time, but described as a merchant when taking out a mortgage the next year, perhaps a step up in the world. It is this man's signature that occurs on a pane of glass in a sash of the addition. Presumably the Dorittys added the lean-to across the rear. In 1892 the Bishop family purchased the property and held it for over seventy years.

Experiences in recent preservation work recounted in the Preface indicate how puzzling such an apparently simple house can be and how the unravelling of changes contradicts conjecture – even by fairly familiar eyes.

The original house was a two-storey four-bay front with off-centre door, gable roof, a large chimney towards the north end. Exterior detail is simple, but the cornice gutter has been restored. The bay window is a picturesque concession to necessity.

The plan of the earlier part has a narrow entrance hall with straight stair and, originally, large rooms on either side the full depth of the building, that to the right or south end possibly intended to be divided into front parlour with the larger and more elaborate windows, and hall bedchamber behind. The large room to the left of the hall had a wainscoat partition cutting off a small space at the back, but the room was probably a family room such as a keeping room, heated by a fireplace, whereas the room across the hall had a stove. In the north end of the house is a large kitchen with cooking hearth and bakeoven reconstructed from the scant evidence of outlines that had survived.

Curiously the house, although allowing for two normal storey heights, was framed to provide an extra foot in height on the ground floor, and a compensating foot less than normal above, while the kitchen is two steps down or ten feet from floor to ceiling! Other curious compromises occur such as the stair with obviously one step too few to make the treads slope forward; taking into account the original stovepipe position across the hall, determined by the location of stone thimbles in the partitions, it is obvious that with the right number of steps bumped heads and scorching hair might have been hazards.

Upstairs the plan was in part a curious ensuite arrangement where the long best bedroom over the keeping room filled the depth of the house, and was heated by a fireplace. This room communicated to another over the front corner, while a separate room opened off the hall at the top of the stairs. Two small bedrooms in the north end were reached by a steep back stair from the kitchen.

The keeping room mantelpiece survives, a very simple design with fluted pilasters, and some of the upper floor four-panel doors, and trim downstairs. The building was also a private school for a time, but in the 1870s a lodging house is recorded, and the official count of thirteen rooms supports this. Over the years many minor changes have occurred but by judicious handling and sympathetic treatment much of the earlier character is being restored.

48

Moore-Bishop-Stokes House

CIRCA 1828

244 King street

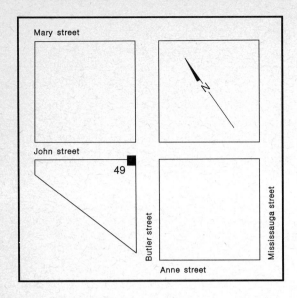

This, another small house, illustrates the variety of early buildings still to be found in Niagara-on-the-Lake. However, it stands outside the main area of the community, on the way to Butler's Burial Ground. From its curious position, straddling a disused right of way, it is suspected that the house was built some time before this part of the town was opened up and on land that was then just a farm. However, checking deeds does not indicate any earlier date for its construction than 1835.

Two other houses resemble it, the Dover-Daly House (46) on Platoff and the early part of the MacMonigle-Craik House (25) on Gate. Like the latter originally, the small fireplace and chimney are on the south side of the Stewart-Anderson House, an unusual position, for north or west were the preferred locations on the colder sides of the building. Here the fireplace back protruded through the frame, flush with the exterior but exposed to view: a very early feature. The house is a saltbox shape with rear lean-to and side extension also with a shed roof in lean-to form.

The arrangement differs from that of the Dover-Daly House with front door which leads to a single large room occupying the ground floor of the main house, this with a fireplace, with the lean-to serving as additional space, and latterly kitchen, as well as giving access via a narrow steep stair to the loft above the front section. Additional bedrooms occupy the ground floor extension.

Some original details survive, in trim including a chair rail, a six-panel door to the front with a finely moulded carcass, parts of sash, and some early hardware. Preservation is assured as a labour of love by the owner.

49

Stewart-Anderson House

CIRCA 1835

507 Butler street

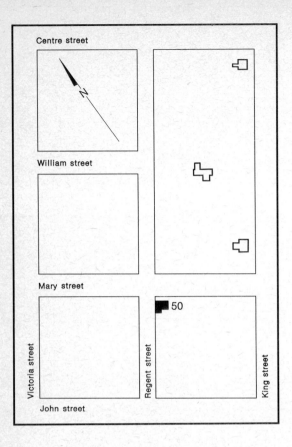

In 1816 the Miller House, home of William Duff Miller, stationer, elder of St Andrew's Church, and officer in the militia, was under construction, for allusion is made in a letter to its nearing completion to be ready the following year. Such is the value of documentation that this house, like the dated Post House (29), is one of the touchstones of local design. Its position, curiously remote from the main centre now, was conveniently mid-way between Queen street and the Court House of 1817, Mr Miller's worlds. For he had also been coroner, registrar, county clerk, inspector and deputy clerk of the crown and pleas.

The house is the simple, five-bay, storey-and-a-half gable form with massive end chimneys. The stacks carry the flues from seven fireplaces, those originally serving to keep the house warm in winter. Externally the detail is almost non-existent with simple moulded cornice and eaves returns and a plain doorway with a transom sash above.

Internally the plan is another variant on the centre hall theme. In the Miller House the hall has a narrow straight flight stair with plain balustrade and square newels with caps. To the right is a long room with large fireplace across the end, a cooking hearth certainly, yet adorned with a graceful mantel, executed with finely reeded detail, which would befit a parlour. This would have been the general family room or keeping room where most daily activity took place, including cooking and dining. In one corner was a cupboard similarly treated with reeding to serve as storage for china and lesser wares. To the left are two rooms each heated by a small corner fireplace. The layout upstairs is four rooms, also with corner fireplaces.

The house preserved most of its early trim including doorcases, doors, chair rails, and baseboards. The mantelpieces survive except for one and there the outline of the trim could be discerned. The smaller mantels are variants of the trim or architrave surround with super-

imposed shelf. Many of the profiles common to the period 1815–25 are represented in this house: hence its value for comparison.

Contrary to the modern notion, such small houses were distinctly formal and treated accordingly, no matter how simple the detail or confined the space. Painted woodwork was the rule and rooms were plastered throughout, the structure usually carefully concealed from view or, if exposed, as occasionally occurs in kitchen wings, generally ornamented to give a neater appearance.

50

The Miller-Taylor House

1817

46 Mary street

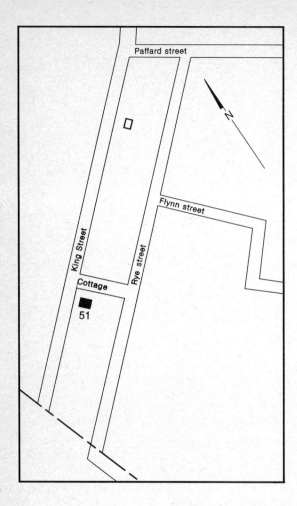

This house was part of the Western Home for Girls, familiarly known as the Rye Home when the old Court House was used as an orphanage, but it was not always part of the establishment. Its design, however, was obviously influenced by its imposing neighbour, and possibly it was built by the same craftsmen. The house is a single storey, the arcaded detail similar to the Court House itself, and a charming example of this local design.

If the interior of this small house is any indication of the grandeur of the Court House itself, then Niagara lost a truly remarkable building for the detail of these rooms, especially the parlour, shows the carpenter-joiner's excellence. However, the building is minimal in its space, a long narrow passage for a hall, a parlour to the left with fireplace, and a tiny slip room behind, and a dining parlour and kitchen on the right, each having a corner fireplace with simple mantelpiece. There is now a rear wing, although this is a later extension to adapt the building for the Rye Home; an earlier appendage must have served as a woodshed.

The tour de force is the parlour, resplendent in all the delicate detail of the early post-War years. A fireplace stands in the centre of the end wall, its mantelpiece gloriously decorated with fluted pilasters of oval shape supporting caps emblazoned with ellipses carved with fluted fans, a centre panel similarly ornamented, and returns around the chimney to match the front, supporting a moulded shelf of intricate outline. Further decoration includes the functional necessities of baseboard and chair rail, but the mitred doorcases are surmounted by overdoors and cornices, the edge of the ceiling ornamented with a wooden cornice, all delicately executed in fine profiles, banded reeding, and slight dentils, fit for a king, with a taste for the period. The interior detail is unsuspected from such a simple exterior: the joy is repeated in like fashion in the Butler House (23), which is equally surprising to the beholder who may once have been the unwitting passer-by.

51

Cameron-Farren House

CIRCA 1817

708 King street

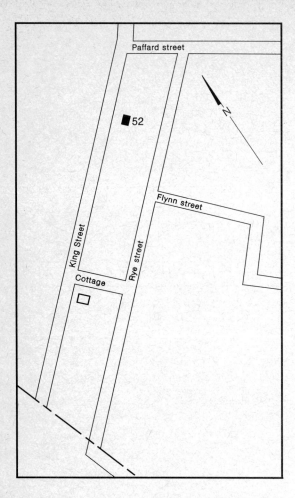

The earliest date referred to, and this on the authority of Janet Carnochan, for this centre chimney house of squared log, is 1816, although the land on which it was built was not sold to George Young by Walter Dickson until 1822. It is the only log dwelling known in the town, but, like several of the buildings of Fort George, and the Men's Quarters of Butler's Barracks, it had a military precedent, for its builder had been for many years master carpenter with the forces. Originally the log with dovetailed corners was exposed, but as it deteriorated it was covered. The house is not far from the old Court House at the end of King street but now appears in the outer fringe of town near the border of the later settlement of 'Irishtown' in the southeast sector.

The log structure might suggest a pre-War building, of the very beginnings of the town, but it is equally conceivable that this was the material of convenience at hand to the builder, was salvaged, or was considered easier to construct. The wood used is various, with many of the logs of the local buttonwood, sometimes known as sycamore or plane tree.

The original form of the building is preserved, and miraculously the centre chimney stack still exists with its four fireplaces and three mantelpieces, one never being so adorned apparently. However, the rear wing has disappeared, but an old photograph records its cooking fireplace, bakeoven, and built-in cupboards.

In layout the centre chimney requires a small box hall leading into the principal rooms on either side of it. Smaller spaces, probably slip rooms, once existed behind these, entered from the main rooms, with a back passage communicating with the wing and a stair to the upper floor where there are two large bedrooms. There is little room for the 'school,' which Miss Young is stated to have been running here in the mid 1820s, but frequently such an establishment had very few pupils,

the arrangement being closer to a private tutorship.

The detail of the house is not very elaborate, except for the mantelpieces of the ground floor where the designs incorporate curious pilasters tapered toward the base, a distinctly eighteenth century shape emanating from the Georgian tradition. One mantel has a cornice developed from the Greek, with metopes and bold guttae, a very odd and unique local design. This joinery suggests an earlier tradition, definitely pre-War; perhaps it came from an older building as salvage or was saved from the Burning, but perhaps it speaks of a craftsman trained long before.

Here there is a curious coincidence in the petition of George Young, late master carpenter of Fort George, who in 1815 sought a pension. In this he refers to his employment as a carpenter in His Majesty's Service since 1776, and suffering great hardship after being taken prisoner in 1813: 'Thus your Petitioner after having exhausted the morning of Life and Strength of his days in the service of his Sovereign is now suspended from employ and Pay on account of the debilitated State of his health, left destitute of the means of Procuring subsistence for myself or Providing for a numerous female family, who by the dearest affections of the soul are entitled to a claim upon him for support.' He was in fact granted a pension of seven shillings and sixpence army sterling and one ration of provisions per day for his pay and allowance.

52

Miss Young's School

1816

630 King street

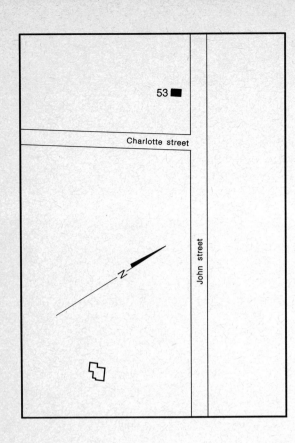

Built on part of the extensive Dickson estates which included the houses Woodlawn (54) and Rowanwood, now demolished, the Dickson-Potter House appears to be built on a small holding purchased by Thomas Barron in 1867. The building may well have been constructed as one of the cottages of the Dickson estate. Nearby still stands a barn finished similarly in board and batten.

Chosen for its secluded charm as well as being representative of the smaller mid Victorian house of the town, this building is reminiscent of the Dover-Daly House (46), similarly finished, and other small centre-door buildings of a storey and a half. The setting is its particular delight with the approach across the upper reaches of One Mile Creek, here diverted into a ditch, under drooping trees and past nestling mounds of gently pungent box.

The dormers are in keeping and the porch part of the total effect, a mid Victorian cottage formally arranged but distinctly picturesque with the traces of the Gothique and the board and batten cladding so beloved of the cottage ornée. The interior is simple and without pretense, a workable layout of larger front room, two smaller ones to the side, and a kitchen in the back ell.

53

Dickson-Potter House

CIRCA 1860

94 John street

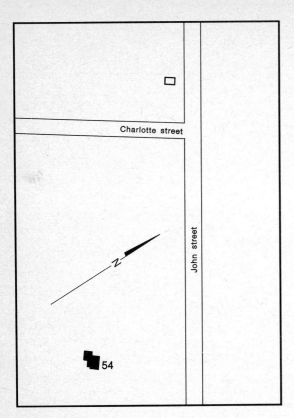

Charlotte street

John street

54

54

Dickson-Rand House

CIRCA 1825 *Randwood*

120 John street

This house typifies, in the grand manner, the adaptation of a dwelling of the early nineteenth century to satisfy the demands of later Victorian and Edwardian times when families made Niagara-on-the-Lake their summer homes. Still easily recognized, the nucleus of the present house was built by the Honourable William Dickson, eminent citizen of Niagara, who is remembered also for his work in the settlement of Dumfries township in Canada Company lands between 1826 and 1835 and the establishment of Galt. Dickson was born in Scotland, coming to Upper Canada in 1785, to build the first brick house in Niagara, and possibly in the province, about 1794. He was a lawyer, justice and clerk of the peace, judge of the district court, and member of the legislative council.

The Honourable William Dickson had built two substantial brick houses before the War, and had apparently lost both in the burning of Niagara: he notes that over 100,000 bricks were available from the ruins. His war losses claim also includes reference to the destruction of his library of over a thousand volumes. Dickson was a man of wealth and position, a much respected citizen of Niagara whose death in 1846 evoked great tribute not only in his own town but in the young but prospering community of Galt.

Within the present great pile the earliest elements are the centre piece with the entrance doorcase adorned with sidelights and fanlight and flanked by a single window on each side: a two-storey brick house with end chimneys.

By the 1870s Niagara-on-the-Lake had become a fashionable resort, and the Dickson estate was an obvious candidate for a family's summer retreat. By the 1880s the roof had been changed to the present mansard form, and various additions were made subsequently. Around the turn of the century the 1880 tower addition had been extended to become a belvedere. Many of the older trees probably date from Dickson's time but the

landscape as we now see it with its long avenue and sunken pool is a contribution by the Rand family in more recent times.

The interior still retains some of the early features such as the layout of the older part with its centre hall, double drawing room to the left and another reception room to the right. Some early joinery survives too in trim and mantelpieces, and it is possible that part of the plasterwork is also original. But later adaptation and modification has been in the Victorian and Edwardian manner, commodious, grand, and epitomizing a leisured life with a well-organized household looked after by faithful retainers: a tug, the summons of a distant bell down the passage, countless footsteps ... and all in order. There is an aura about this house and others like it that brings back the very atmosphere of an age not long ago.

Yet another fascinating house with a similar background stands in the grounds of the estate to the east; 'Brunswick Place,' was originally built by Captain Robert Melville, an important functionary in the Niagara Harbour and Dock Company which was incorporated in 1831 and became a major industry in the mid-nineteenth century, to collapse a short time later.

Melville built his fine two-storey brick house in 1831. This is a three-bay design with elaborate centre doorcase much ornamented with mouldings, fanlight, sidelights, and colonnettes. The wide windows have intermediate posts or vertical mullions dividing them into a full light at the centre, and a half light at each side, an arrangement very similar to the Lyons-Jones House (58) built shortly after. As at Randwood, subsequent embellishment and enlargement of the house commenced in the 1880s and continued well into this century.

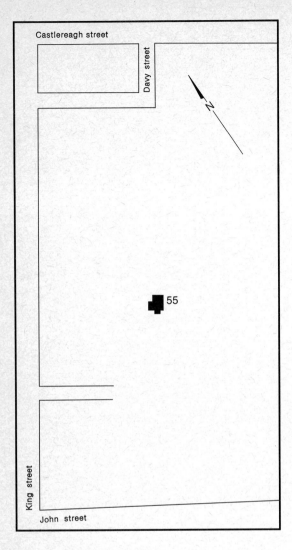

Castlereagh street

Davy street

N

55

King street

John street

55

Commissariat's Quarters

CIRCA 1817

Military Reserve

Only four buildings survive of the extensive complex of military structures known as Butler's Barracks. Between Fort George and Butler's Barracks two other early buildings once stood: the Commandant's Quarters burnt in 1880 and the Indian Council House which later became a hospital razed in a fire of 1858; archaeologists have recently been investigating their remains.

Although the establishment known as Butler's Barracks is named after Butler's Rangers and its leader, Colonel John Butler, the present buildings are now believed to be post-War, the earliest date recorded being 1817. An earlier group of 'Rangers Barracks' is shown on a pre-War map on low lying land amounting to swamp near the water's edge, not far from the present Dock Area; it may have been this unhealthy situation which brought approbrium to Colonel Butler's older quarters.

Postcards, until recently still available, also showed a range of single storey Officers' Barracks, removed only a few decades ago. Butler's Barracks has been reduced to four buildings: the Men's Quarters, its lower storey of squared log and its upper storey of frame, brick-filled; a gun shed or storehouse, a long frame building of a single storey; a two-storey frame storehouse or workshop; and the low verandahed cottage referred to as the Commissariat's Quarters.

This last building is a typical Niagara form with large interior chimneys, a single storey with gable end and three openings across the front. The low encircling verandah gives a somewhat disarming and diminutive scale to the building, an appearance too of still being Imperially British to the core. Curiously, however, this is a later addition and an old photograph shows it with a small vestibule very similar to the one replaced on the Creen House on Simcoe street. The interior, however, is typically local and rather simple. Extensions to the rear probably housed kitchens and stores for the military establishment.

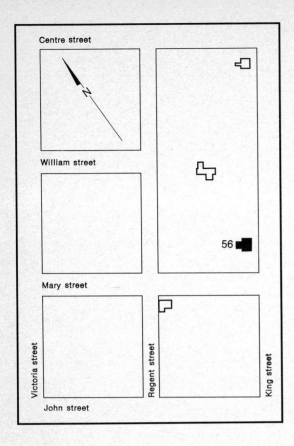

This building has been more recently known as 'Brockamour,' the allusion being to John Powell's sister-in-law, Sophia Shaw, believed to be Brock's fiancée, who had been staying in the Powell's summer house on the River road nearer Queenston. References in correspondence mention making do in a kitchen wing, which suggests that part of the original house survived the holocaust of 1813. John Powell was registrar of the county, a highly respected citizen of the community, who died in 1826, but whose family continued in the house until 1836. It was owned next by James Boulton, barrister.

The walls of this house are finished in stucco, jointed to simulate cut stone, a not uncommon pretence in the Regency and the corresponding period in Upper Canada. However, this finish conceals brick which, as the house faces the devastating east winds, may have required this protective treatment. The house is a typical form, two storeys in height, a three-bay front, with hipped roof and interior chimneys. The extraordinary width of the windows, giving fifteen panes over fifteen in the upper floor, is similar to the Post House (29) where slightly larger glass was used.

Downstairs later changes have occurred, and the glass has been altered too. The bracketted cornice approaches that on the Court House of 1847 and indicates refurbishing about this time. Some time in the 1840s a large ballroom with nursery over it was added to the northwest corner which may account for the additional entrance and the present position of the stair in a side hall at the back of the house: the ballroom wing has since been demolished.

The interior does preserve some original detail or manifestations of the earlier changes but more recent fires and later alterations have seen the disappearance of part of the building's character.

56

Powell-Cavers House

CIRCA 1818

433 King street

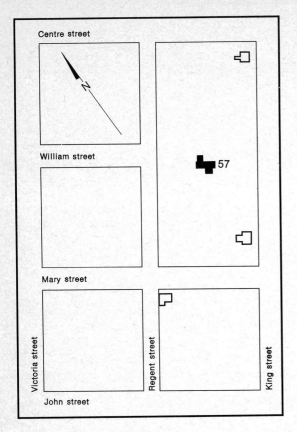

What a joy to grow up in a 'wilderness' right in the middle of town! This four-acre property was presented to the widow of Daniel Claus by the Indians who so admired and respected her late husband as their agent and supporter. Daniel Claus, one of the Loyalists who died in Britain in 1789 seeking redress for his losses in the American war, was succeeded by his son William as deputy superintendent of Indian affairs, a man much interested in the area, especially in the cultivation of tender fruit trees such as nectarines and peaches in the locality. One Mile Creek meanders through the property which is still covered by immense trees including one huge oak, and enclosed along King street by a magnificent row of majestic buttonwoods. The stump of a balm of Gilead still marks the remains of the stately landmark used for years by navigators on the lake.

In the burning of 1813 the old house which stood on top of the creek bank was lost. Records indicate that a portion of the present house was being lived in by 1816 and this is known to be that to the right of the front door, now the library, and that in 1817 an addition was being put up to match it on the left. Further extensions were made shortly afterwards.

William Claus kept extensive diaries while building the 'cottage' as he called it; some of his many interests are indicated in this excerpt: 'April 29th (1817) ... Began to draw Bricks from Mr. Dickson's kiln for the bedroom — put up pailing round the well to prevent the children from falling by climbing. Dug a boarder under the bedroom window & set out several rose bushes and tulips, narcissus and one hyacinth. Sowed sweet peas and other flower seed ...' References to his work on his fruit trees and vines are intermingled with comments on housebuilding, materials, and the prices of labour.

This one-storey rambling bungalow nestles in its wilderness like a contented bird, almost camouflaged by greenery, and hidden from the street. In the spring the grounds are carpetted with daffodils and squills, in early summer the woods are redolent with the scent of the mauve and milky mist of dame's violet's flowers. Sweet-scented black locust and opulent catalpas are now part of the ornamentals.

The exterior is stucco, lined as for stone, over brickwork: the original finish may have been similar. The doorway is decorated with a fanlight. The chimneys push through the hip roof to serve interior fireplaces, a common plan. The hall is central to the main block, the room on the right is the library but earlier was possibly a parlour or drawing room. The fireplace here has beside it curiously devised alcoves, curved in plan with reeded reveals, forming cupboards, the heads with a somewhat pointed ellipse, the opposite 'cut' of the usual shape, with keystones set at the top. To the left is another sitting room and a dining room beyond which was formerly a bedroom, with the present kitchen behind the drawing room replacing an earlier one to the west. The bedrooms are off in the wing. Trim elsewhere is relatively plain with simple four-panel doors, flush and beaded on one side as reminders of the early post-War reconstruction.

57

The Wilderness
CIRCA 1816

407 King street

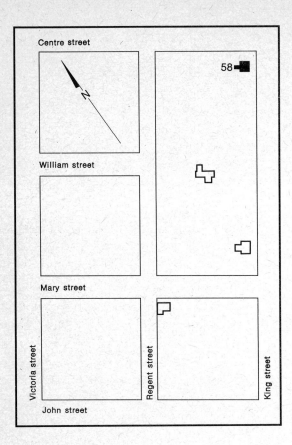

The acre lot on which this house stands was owned by a Mrs Geale, one of the Claus family who lived next door at the Wilderness. In the year 1835 it was made over to John Lyons, a lawyer and registrar of the county of Lincoln, who married Mrs Geale. The ceiling cornice in the drawing room is identical to that in the Post House of 1835 (29), yet further corroboration for the date of this house. But here the similarity ceases.

Unlike most early houses of the town this is set back from the street, and surrounded by a garden where many old fashioned favourites like crown imperials, feather leaved 'pinnies,' Star of Bethlehem, martagon lilies, lilac, and cabbage roses appeared year after year despite neglect. Even a white wisteria clung to the dilapidated late Victorian porch that latterly disguised the entrance front.

The outward form is the common two-storey building over a high basement, with hipped roof and end chimneys, but its design is distinctly out of the ordinary. The roughcast over masonry is a typical Regency wall finish; a watercolour sketch c1845 shows this house white, and it was presumably so treated. The large side windows, broken into a centre piece with sidelights, and with folding shutters, light the principal rooms. But the most fascinating feature, and pure Regency deceit, is the treatment of the blind windows on the entrance front made to resemble shuttered openings just to balance the design of the façade: behind stand fireplace and chimney stack! The doorway is notable with its eight-panelled door deeply fielded and moulded, much divided sidelights, and well proportioned fanlight. The side wing is an addition and the coachhouse a recent structure.

The plan has a side hall, generously scaled, an elegant stair with scrolled handrail, and a small room at the end. The drawing room is to the left, the dining room behind, interconnected to each other and to the hall. Downstairs was the basement kitchen, its cooking fireplace on the wall of the entrance front, originally with storerooms and servants' room behind. Upstairs there were two large bedrooms similar in size to the reception rooms downstairs, a smaller bedroom over the front door and a dressing room leading from the upper hall at the head of the stair and connected to the adjoining bedroom. The newer side wing now serves as modern domestic offices.

In other ways the house is somewhat strange, for there is an obvious hankering after the older fashion of symmetrical pilastered trims and a desire to keep up with the newer fashion of the Greek Revival. The result is a curious and, to some, rather clumsy compromise, with extraordinarily heavy and complicated doorcases with roundel corner blocks. The effect is grand, matched to some degree by the plaster cornices and the remains of the hall rosette but slightly at variance with the more delicate staircase. The mantelpieces in the principal rooms are of wood, but fashioned almost to resemble marble, with the traditional motifs of fans lightly incised rather than in bas-relief with the shelf above of intricately curved outline.

The house is curiously similar to the building known as the Grange on Brown street in Port Hope, built by a lawyer named Smith about 1832. Odd that the form and original plan should correspond, and that similar, but not identical, conceits of blocked windows should be practised: perhaps the coincidence is the result of more than a nodding acquaintance.

58

Lyons-Jones House

CIRCA 1835

8 Centre street

Selective bibliography

This does not attempt to be an exhaustive bibliography, for there are many books, particularly those of early travellers, which allude to Niagara. The titles in the list were selected to indicate further reading for those who are interested in particular aspects of the background of the area.

Annals of Niagara
William Kirby
Toronto: Macmillan Co. of Canada Ltd., 1927
A more general and very readable account of the history of Niagara, republished in a version edited by Lorne Pierce. Now out of print.

*The First History of the Freedom
of Worship in the Town and Township
of Niagara 1640–1962*
Frances MacKay
Sketches by David Low. Published by arrangement with the Niagara Town and Township Chamber of Commerce, Virgil, Ontario: Niagara Press
A fascinating account of the churches and burial grounds of the area, very much in order for reprinting in an up-to-date revised edition.

History of Niagara
Janet Carnochan
Toronto: William Briggs, 1914
The most extensive history of old Niagara on the Lake and as such the most useful, although some statements have not been borne out by later research. It suffers from two major drawbacks, a lack of footnotes quoting the authority or sources of information and a calm assumption that those who read it are thoroughly familiar with the town at the time of writing, 1914. Almost sixty years has changed the context. Unfortunately now out of print.

The War of 1812 on the Niagara Frontier
Louis L. Babcock
Buffalo, New York: Buffalo Historical Society, 1927
An American account of the War mainly as it affected the frontier, but with a just and balanced account of the affairs at Niagara.

For general enjoyment and further background the following form a useful, but by no means comprehensive list of those publications still available in the original or reprinted form, or readily found in most public libraries.

The Ancestral Roof
Anthony Adamson and Marion MacRae
Toronto: Clarke, Irwin, & Co. Ltd., 1963.
A wide subject broadly painted and often brightly so, but an enjoyable introduction to the subject of building in Ontario.

At Home in Upper Canada
Jeanne Minhinnick
Toronto: Clarke, Irwin, & Co. Ltd., 1970
The social background, filling in the story of life in Ontario's earlier years; a companion book to any appreciation of building in the province, by one whose study and sympathy has cast so much light on the interpretation of this story.

*Early Architecture of the Town
and Township of Niagara*
Peter John Stokes
Niagara: Niagara Foundation, 1967
A limited edition of an illustrated glossary, based mostly on the experience of the Niagara Pilot Study for the National Inventory of Building, giving considerable architectural detail.

Niagara
Ralph Greenhill and Thomas D. Mahoney
Toronto: University of Toronto Press, 1969
A fascinating history of the local wonder of the world, the Falls of Niagara, with many illustrations to document the development of that great attraction.

Rural Ontario
Verschoyle Benson Blake and Ralph Greenhill
Toronto: University of Toronto Press, 1969
An invaluable, enjoyable, and authoritative background to the province's origins, its settlement, and its architecture as represented still in the rural scene, finely illustrated.

Winter Studies and Summer Rambles in Canada
Anna Brownell Jameson
Toronto: McClelland and Stewart Ltd., 1965
New Canadian Library No. 46
The vivid impressions, coloured perhaps by disappointments, of a visitor from England in the late 1830s.

The following are out of print, but are
sometimes available in reference libraries.

A Century of Sail and Steam
on the Niagara River
Barlow Cumberland
Toronto: Musson Book Co. Ltd., 1913

The Diary of Mrs John Graves Simcoe
Edited by John Ross Robertson
Toronto: William Briggs, 1911
A fascinating account, originally illustrated with
sketches by the author of life in the beginning
of Upper Canada and on travels through the
wilderness of the new colony.

The Early Buildings of Ontario
Eric R. Arthur
Toronto: University of Toronto Press, 1938

The History of Freemasonry in Canada
John Ross Robertson
Toronto: Hunter Rose, 1899

Small Houses of the Late Eighteenth
and Early Nineteenth Centuries in Ontario
Eric R. Arthur
Toronto: University of Toronto Press, 1927,
for the Department of Architecture and the
School of Engineering Research

Pamphlets by the Niagara Historical
Society, published prior to 1940.

Glossary

It is often most helpful to visualize the total
building first, but it is equally important, and
just as enjoyable, to feast one's eyes upon the
various details which differentiate each composite and contribute to its essential character.
This glossary has been compiled as an aid to
that detail; the arrangement is a reasonable
progression from the general to the particular,
sweeping from eye level upwards.

Various details are grouped to allow comparison, for it is only by this method that one can
appreciate the development of decoration and
the elaboration often practised, as well as the
subtle differences which also occur from building to building. Not only is the richness of the
material to be seen focussed in the camera's
spyglass, but the harmonious variety possible
within the discipline of tradition is also revealed.
This order means that examples of one period
have been separated. It helps to command our
respect for the accomplishment of those who
built before us.

The illustrations for the glossary are details of
photographs taken for this book by Philip
Shackleton.

 McKee-Dodson   Crysler-Rigg   Creen   Barker Hall

DOORWAYS

From the simple and unadorned requirement of an entrance with the conventional panelled door, doorways became the principal subject for elaboration on the exterior displaying all the skill that the joiner and glazier could muster. The examples show the variety of detail employed in such adornment.

Simple Architrave
The doorway of the McKee-Dodson House (2) has a simple surround of moulded trim and a six-panelled door with the topmost panels glazed to help light the hall.

Decorative Architrave
Still only a doorcase, but on the Crysler-Rigg (Roslyn Cottage) (15) it has the other extreme of elaboration, with intricate moulding and detail in the Greek Revival taste.

Simple Architrave with Transom
The door on the Creen House (20) is functionally similar to the McKee-Dodson House (2), but it has a light (or sash) above a transom bar incorporated into a design of comparable simplicity.

Architrave with Transom and Colonettes
Barker Hall (32) displays a more elaborate design with deep reveals, and colonettes supporting the transom bar treated here as a cornice.

Breakenridge-Ure

Kerr-Wooll

Promenade House

Barker Hall

Gollop

Post House

Transoms

The transom here refers to the rectangular light or sash in the upper part of a divided opening. In the Breakenridge-Ure House (18) the transom has a rectilinear design of glass panes, further subdivided by intermediate pilasters of the doorcase, while the Kerr-Wooll House (5) heralds the preference for the fan motif. Intricate patterns of lozenges were also worked out in curved cames of thin metal ornamented with lead rosettes represented by the Promenade House (4), and the simpler diamond arrangement of interlocking wood glazing bars of Barker Hall (32).

Doorcase with Sidelights and Cornice

The Gollop House (12) represents one of the typical doorcases seen on frame houses in Niagara; its treatment, with the high frieze board, elaborate cornice, and moulded pilasters at the sides, is somewhat reminiscent of mantelpieces. The sidelights beside the door give light to the centre hall.

Doorcase with Fanlight

In the Post House (29) the doorway is the most important opening, ornamented with stone impost blocks and a keystone, the doorcase itself having moulded pilasters and a fanlight.

Lockhart-Moogk

Rogers-Harrison

Breakenridge-Ure

MacDougal-Harrison

Breakenridge-Hawley

Jones-Eckersley-Brownell

Lyons-Jones

With Sidelights and Transom
The treatment in the Lockhart-Moogk House (22) is similar to the Breakenridge-Ure House (18), but slightly simpler with sidelights to the top of the door and a transom light across the whole width of the doorway. Some of the glazing bars or muntins have been lost from the transom.

With Sidelights and Fanlight
Perhaps the most elaborate treatment occurs in the examples of this very popular design; the semi-elliptical top light and sidelights are embroidered to become an intricate web of cames, swags, and rosettes. The Rogers-Harrison House (13) shows a simpler version in metal while the MacDougal-Harrison (14) is the ultimate in complexity, almost defying description. A nice balance occurs in the elaboration of the Breakenridge-Hawley House (19) where the doorcase itself commands as much attention in a design reminding one of detail of the Federal Period in New England. The Jones-Eckersley-Brownell House (31) shows in wood a return to the fan

pattern further illustrated in the Lyons-Jones House (58) where the rectilinear design of sidelights and boldly moulded door represents the period 1835–45.

MacDougal-Harrison

Richardson-Kiely

Post House

MacDougal-Harrison   Barker Hall

Breakenridge-Hawley

Lyons-Jones

Breakenridge-Hawley

Details

Fans or fanlights already illustrated as parts of the doorcases above are worthy of closer scrutiny. The MacDougal-Harrison House (14) exhibits the greatest confusion and contrasts with the directness of the Richardson-Kiely House (16), or the ordered intricacy of the Breakenridge-Hawley House (19). The Post House (29) shows again a simple fan in a semicircle, while the Lyons-Jones House (58) is a flat semi-ellipse.

A *sidelight*, here from the MacDougal-Harrison House (14) is, as its name implies, set beside the door to help light the hall beyond.

The *transom bar* is the horizontal member of a doorcase above the door itself and separating it from the upper light of the doorway. In Barker Hall (32) this is elaborately treated as an entablature supported by colonettes and surmounted by a small cornice.

The *cornice*, here part of the doorcase in the Breakenridge-Hawley House (19), is the top projecting member supported by brackets usually called modillions.

Crysler-Rigg

Barker Hall

Carlisle-Brook

Court House

Lyons-Jones

Court House

Rogers-Harrison

Barker Hall

WINDOWS

Door panels, the intermediate wood sections fitted into a frame or carcass to form the door itself, are frequently ornamented with raised centres called fielding and surrounded with panel moulds as in the extremely elaborate treatment of the Crysler-Rigg House (15). That of Barker Hall (32) with bolection or raised moulds to panels and elaborate fielding resembles that in the Lyons-Jones House (58), while the Court House (37) shows a much bolder treatment applied to a civic building.

Vestibules and *porches* are those accoutrements put over the entrance to a building for protection from the weather. The vestibule in the Carlisle-Brook House (28) is reputed to have been moved from the Vanderlip-Marcy House (29). In the Court House (37) the porch is a fine essay in stone by William Thomas.

Ornament and *furniture* covers the unusual detail of doorways such as the keystone in wood on the Rogers-Harrison House (13) and the hardware represented by the fine knocker inscribed 'Barker Hall' in (32).

Divided Sash
The vertically sliding window in two lights or sashes is the most common form in early Canadian building and was much used throughout colonial North America. It is typical of English architecture in the late seventeenth century, having been inherited from the Dutch at the time of William and Mary. The casement or hinged sash is less frequent and occurs seldom in Niagara. Frequently the upper sash was fixed, and only the lower one opened; with an odd number of panes vertically, the smaller sash is usually at the bottom as in the McKee-Dodson House (2), in contrast to the double hung sash of Georgian and Regency England. Because

McKee-Dodson

MacDougal-Harrison   Powell-Cavers

Whale Inn

Richardson-Kiely   Clench

Carlisle-Brook   Sign of the Pineapple

glass was difficult to make in large sheets by early hand methods, it was cut into small stock sizes and packed into cases. Therefore, the sash fits the glass, rather than the pane being cut from a large sheet to fit the sash as in modern times. The old practice is represented in the MacDougal-Harrison House (14) where sashes of twelve over twelve give the familiar twenty-four paned window and in the Powell-Cavers House (56) with no less than thirty panes! As its manufacturing improved glass became cheaper and of better quality, with fewer blemishes, and available in larger sizes so that the number of panes in a sash decreased as the period advanced as seen in the Whale Inn (40).

Divided Windows
Particular windows of distinctive character frequently have the names of architects or places attached to them – for example, that over the entrance of the Richardson-Kiely House (16) known as Palladian (after Andrea Palladio) or Venetian with its centre piece arched and sidelights flat headed, while the plainer form with straight head, shown in the Clench House (23), was sometimes known as a Wyatt window presumably after James Wyatt (1746–1813), the architect.

Windows with Shutters
Shutters, referred to as early as 1827 in Joseph Pickering's remarks on Venetian blinds, are a characteristic feature of Niagara houses, and in the Carlisle-Brook House (28) the louvres or slats are fixed, yet those in The Sign of the Pineapple (38) are movable allowing light and ventilation to be controlled at will. Solid shutters with panels are also seen.

14

St Andrew's Church   Court House   Niagara Apothecary

Rectory   St Mark's Church   Sherlock Block

WALLS

Special Shapes

In important buildings the window became a subject for elaboration too and in St Andrew's Church (20) a remarkable form with semi-circular head and fan has treble-hung sash each of twenty-four panes. The Court House (37) represents an architect's approach to the lighting of the stair landing leading to the court room. The Italianate splendour of the Rectory (41) is illustrated by a variety of window shapes ornamenting the tower of this Tuscan villa. The window in the vestry of St Mark's Church (42) represents the original divisions of sash prior to later alterations to stained glass elsewhere in the building.

Details

Two shopfront window details are represented in the cable moulding, carved capital and corbel of the head to the Niagara Apothecary (1) and in the arcading of the Sherlock Block (36).

Walls, particularly those of wood, are also surfaces for ornamentation in various classical motifs and occasionally in the romantic fashion; the decoration, however, is usually restrained and sparse.

Although stone is a common local material, the limestone of the Niagara escarpment being only eight miles away, it was seldom used except in foundations or occasionally in carved or cut ornament.

Brunswick Place

Lyons-Jones

Court House

Court House

Kerr-Wooll

Breakenridge-Ure

Rectory

Stonework

The regularly coursed, hammer-dressed stone, and cut and tooled plinth of the Lyons-Jones House (58) is indicative of more carefully constructed walls. Stone was thought appropriate to a fine civic building like the Court House (37) and lent itself to carved ornament like the figurehead for keystone, columns, cornice, and balustrade of the porch and ornamental window heads and cornices above as well as the projecting corner blocks or rusticated quoins set in coursed rubble to the rear entrance. In Brunswick Place (referred to in 54) the delicate tooling of stone quoins to brickwork is very well preserved.

Brickwork

The more common masonry material was brick manufactured from local clay, one brickyard being noted on early maps close to the mouth of One Mile Creek. For added strength brick walls were built in structural patterns called bonds by arranging the brick lengthwise to the face as a 'stretcher' or with its end showing as a 'header.' The most popular, and one of the strongest of these, was Flemish bond seen in the Kerr-Wooll House (5) where stretchers and headers alternate both horizontally and vertically. Because of its obvious expense this was usually reserved for street fronts only and common bond, comprising several rows of stretchers alternating with a row of headers, was used elsewhere. But in the Breakenridge-Ure House (18) common bond is employed on the street fronts too. Stretcher bond, illustrated in the Rectory (41), became a favourite later, particularly as it conserved face brick, here a pressed buff or 'white' variety, and relied upon bond bricks notched in behind the face for strength.

Cameron-Farren

MacDougal-Harrison

Breakenridge-Ure

Kerr-Wooll

Butler

Dickson-Potter

Decorative Arcading: One memorable feature of some Niagara buildings, and following the tradition of the second Court House, is the decorative brick arcading represented in its neighbour, the Cameron-Farren House (51) and best exemplified in the MacDougal-Harrison House (14).

String courses are decorative banding usually associated with floor levels as shown in the Breakenridge-Ure House (18). When these connect sills they are generally described as sill courses, and, when placed at the top of a foundation, as a plinth.

Flat arches with inclined brickwork are self-supporting and the Kerr-Wooll House (5) illustrates the usual practice of spanning relatively narrow openings where a single stone or lintel is not used.

Wood

Wood finishes are common in Niagara where the majority of houses are framed in timber. *Clapboard* is a thin board secured against the frame to overlap that below thus shedding water and keeping the house fairly weathertight (but not always windtight): here in the Butler House (23) it is secured by hand-wrought nails to the vertical planking of the walls.

In the Dickson-Potter House (53) vertical *board and batten* is the covering, another finish much liked in more romantic and picturesque styles like the cottage ornée or the small Gothic Revival villa.

Crysler-Rigg

St Andrew's Church

Clench

Niagara Apothecary

Dee-LeDoux Block

Creen

St Andrew's Church

St Andrew's Church

Rectory

Decorative Treatment

The walls were for the most part plain, but there were decorative features applied, and the principal details require definition.

St Andrew's Church (21) indicates in this partial view a Greek Doric *column* with its beautifully fashioned cap.

The Creen House (20) is a composition in *pediments*, the triangular features above the dormers and porch; the Rectory (41) exhibits a much more florid and bracketted version of the same detail.

Pilasters are one of the details noteworthy in several frame houses in Niagara. In the Crysler-Rigg House (15) the fluted form surmounted by the exquisitely carved ramshorns of the Ionic cap is crowned by a modillion cornice; that in the Clench House (24) is similarly elaborate.

The portico with its surmounting pediment in St Andrew's Church (21) is an excellent essay in the Greek Doric style and here is grafted to a building essentially classical of Renaissance inspiration rather than Greek Revival in character.

Intermediate cornices often occur in shopfront details like that in the Niagara Apothecary (1) which is decidedly of the 1860s whereas that wrought in stone at the Dee-LeDoux Block (34) is more classical in detail and somewhat earlier.

Impost blocks are the haunches or stone blocks below the spring of an arch and are frequently decorated or projecting as in the entrance to St Andrew's Church (21) where the stone arch culminates in a *keystone*.

St Andrew's Church

McClelland's

Post House

Powell-Cavers

Lyons-Jones

Whale Inn

Datestones are unusual features, and are invaluable evidence wherever they occur: in St Andrew's Church (21) 1831 is spelt out in Roman numerals and in the Post House (29) 1835 indicates the date of building.

Stucco is another common finish, often signifying a later change especially on frame buildings where clapboard needs frequent painting and maintenance; in the Powell-Cavers House (56) the stucco is applied to brick and deeply jointed to resemble ashlar or cut stone. In the Lyons-Jones House (58), however, it is roughcast, applied in the Regency tradition as a more picturesque finish to brick; a sketch of the 1840s indicates this house to be white then.

Gable openings often take decorative form as in the semi-elliptical fan above the provisioner's T sign of McClelland's (11) and in the quarter moons lighting the loft of the Whale Inn (40).

Rectory

St Andrew's Church

Court House

Baikie-Borsook

ROOFS

The *verandah* became very popular after 1840; this version in the Baikie-Borsook House (45) was probably built after 1850 with strong leanings to the fretwork ornament of stock Victorian pattern.

Our last and unfortunately often least concern is for the tops of buildings, the ornaments of roofs and details of projections, in former times considered an integral part of the whole.

The base of the roof and its edges – termed *eaves* on the horizontal projection and *verges* on the incline or gable – were usually adorned with ornament to form the *cornice*. In St Andrew's Church (21) the Greek detail includes an entablature decorated with *triglyphs* and intervening larger spaces, normally referred to as *metopes*, above which are representative brackets with *guttae* or drops which are also carried up the slope in the raking cornice. The fluted shafts of the columns terminate in the *echinus* or gently rounded moulding below the square cap or *abacus*. In the Court House (37) the cornice is elaborated with brackets which in the Rectory (41) become even more exaggerated.

Niagara Apothecary

McClelland's

McKee-Dodson

Whale Inn

Davidson-Campbell

Eaves returns are a common feature at the gables of early buildings and from their adopted function are often referred to by carpenters as 'bird houses.' Often these decorative features were combined with *cornice gutters*, even on quite simple houses, where the trough was hollowed out of solid timber moulded along the edge to form the decorative cornice. In the course of years many of these distinctive features were allowed to decay and were never replaced, thus removing part of the building's essential character. In the Niagara Apothecary (1) the eaves return is a development of the lower mouldings of the cornice; in McClelland's (11) the neat termination of stone quoins formed by

the eaves return is most appropriate. The remarkable delicacy of the curved tip of the raking cornice to house the gutter and the fine return is an unexpected pleasure in the McKee-Dodson House (2). The Whale Inn (40) shows the incipient disease: the eaves have been sloped in a later modification whereas the eye can visualize the return extending to the left to form a cornice gutter.

The *bargeboard* is essentially a detail of the picturesque and romantic period best expressed in the Gothic Revival and inspired originally by the carved and fretted ornament of Tudor half-timbered houses. By the time it reaches expression in the Davidson-Campbell House (7) it is somewhat removed from its origins and simplified, but there still is the vestige of a *pendant* or *drop* on the left which should be complemented at the ridge by another drop and a finial above the roof.

Creen

Rectory

Kerr-Wooll

Dickson-Potter

Dickson-Rand

Miller-Taylor

Commissariat

St Andrew's Church

Rectory

The *dormer* is a small window projecting from the roof and usually to light a part storey within the roof space, a place often reserved for sleeping; hence its derivation. In the Creen House (20) a reconstruction in a traditional form is illustrated indicating the characteristic small sash tightly enclosed by wings, a maximum of window to a minimum of wall. The Dickson-Potter House (53) illustrates a later version with similar effect, but also having shutters, an unusual feature. A typical later Victorian detail is shown in the Dickson-Rand House (54).

Even *chimneys*, being necessary and inevitable, were treated with some concern for detail and appearance. Generally chimneys were built higher than we are accustomed to, probably for reasons of safety for sparks could easily ignite a wooden roof. Those in the Rectory (41) are substantial and elaborately contrived in brick with recessed panels and ornamental caps. In the Miller-Taylor House (50) an original stack has survived, a large shaft of handmade brick neatly topped out in corbelled banding, while the Kerr-Wooll House (5) shows a more elaborate version. A hood (Commissariat's Quarters [55]) coped with smoking fireplaces and trees, and also was a spark arrester.

Towers and Steeples
The most noteworthy tower and steeple is that of St Andrew's Church (21) a dignified crown to the building it adorns, with coupled Ionic colonettes across the corner supporting the entablature broken out above them on the upper stage and a simpler lower stage of wood marked to imitate stone detail. More domestic in feeling is the Tuscan tower accenting the Italianate pile of the Rectory (41) with its tiered effect emphasized by band courses and different window treatment.

St Andrew's Church

St Andrew's Church

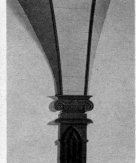

St Vincent de Paul

CHURCHES AND CHURCHYARDS

These are in fact a little apart from our main preoccupation and require some special treatment particularly with reference to the interiors.

The pulpitum executed by John Davidson in 1840 for St Andrew's Church (21). A splendid essay of the joiner's art in the native wood, black walnut.

Turned column, capital, and panelled balustrade of the galleries of St Andrew's, 1831, typical detail of a Classical interior of an early nineteenth century church in Upper Canada.

A breath of the picturesque, or the eclectic, a meeting of romantic and classic worlds in the 1834 interior of the church of St Vincent de Paul (43). The tip of the pilaster ornamented with bold pointed reeding terminated in a Gothic arch sports a cap of Greek inspiration, rather liberally and poetically interpreted from the Ionic, to form the spring of a groined vault finished entirely in wood.

St Mark's Church   St Mark's Church   St Mark's Church   St Mark's Church   St Mark's Church

A tribute to the Reverend Robert Addison, the first man to minister to the Church of England in the parish of Niagara and round about; the memorial tablet in the west end of St Mark's Church (42).

The chancel of St Mark's Church, after the preservation work of 1964, shows the changes made at that time to the 1843 extension to the church and the restoration of the high pulpits, which used to overlook the galleries destroyed in the alterations of 1892.

A church still evolving: the bronze font cover with St Mark and his winged lion by Jacobine Jones, RCA, commissioned in 1964 for St Mark's in memory of Sir Wylie Grier.

The churchyard of St Mark's, having been the earliest burial ground in the town, and prior to 1833 the only one used, is well furnished with fascinating tombstones of the early nineteenth century and one or two even earlier. Besides table tombs and sarcophagi, many of the upright stones illustrate the typical classical shapes, with some joined to form pairs. The lettering and stone cutting on many is particularly fine, for example, that to James Wilson. Several plots are enclosed by cast iron railings, some decidedly classical in inspiration others more Victorian in detail.

Index of buildings

This book
was designed by
Allan Fleming
with the assistance of
Laurie Lewis
and was printed by
University of
Toronto
Press
1971